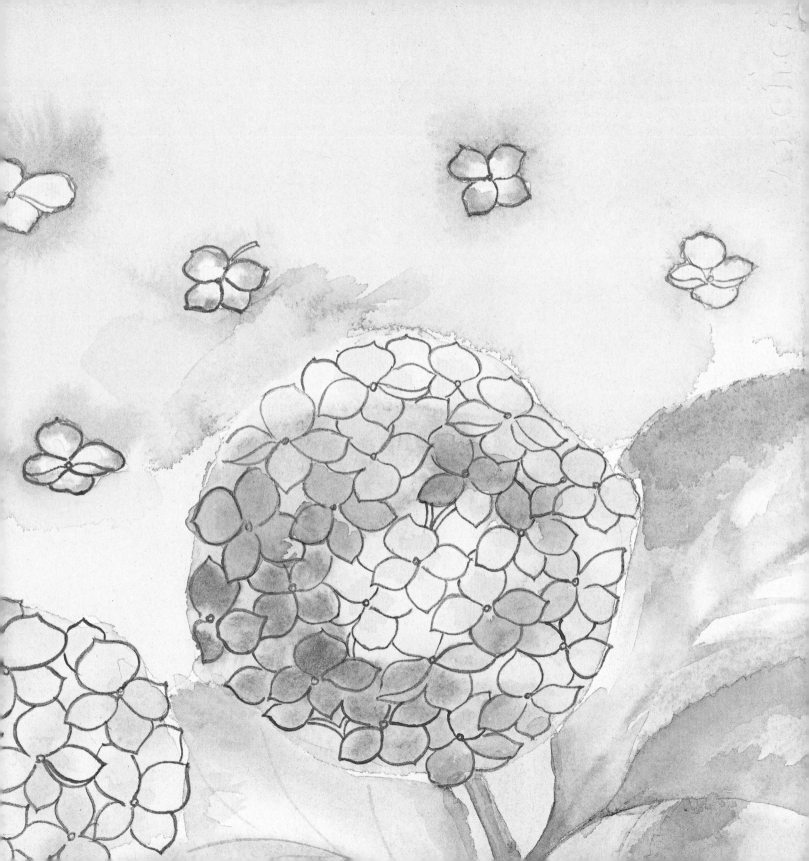

Flower Origami

Fabric Flowers from Simple Shapes

Kumiko Sudo

Breckling Press

Library of Congress Cataloging-in-Publication Data
Sudo, Kumiko.
    Flower origami : fabric flowers from simple shapes / Kumiko Sudo.
—1st ed.
        p. cm.
        ISBN 0-9721218-4-6
        1. Appliqué—Patterns. 2. Quilting—Patterns. 3. Flowers in art. 4. Origami.
I. Title.

    TT779.S8422 2004
    746.44'5—dc22

                                                    2004007353

This book was set in Whitman and Meta by Bartko Design, Inc.
Editorial direction by Anne Knudsen
Cover and interior design by Kim Bartko
Cover and interior photographs by Sharon Hoogstraten
Calligraphy and water color paintings by Kumiko Sudo
Technical drawings by Kandy Petersen

With special thanks to Yuwa Fabric Company and National Non Wovens for their support

Published by Breckling Press
283 N. Michigan St., Elmhurst, IL 60126 USA

Printed and bound in Canada
International Standard Book Number: 0-9721-2184-6

Contents

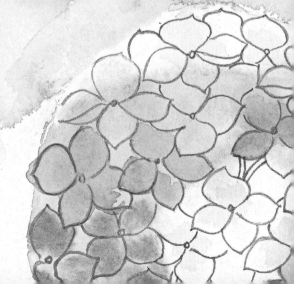

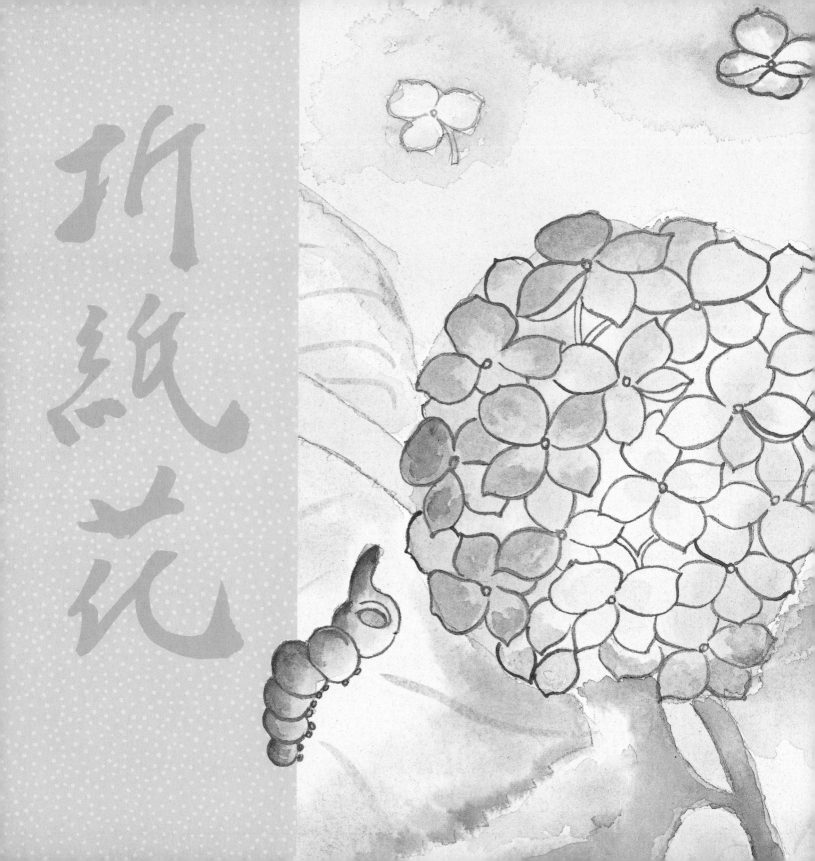

Preface

FLOWERS ARE A THEME that I return to with every quilt or fabric project I make. I am often asked where ideas for new designs come from. My answer is that inspiration requires a deep sensitivity toward the world around us. This means not looking just at nicely trimmed or arranged flowers in flower shops, but at all that nature has to offer. I try to open my eyes to wildflowers that cling to pathways, seedlings ready to fall from withered plants, or tiny clusters of moss on the surface of a tree trunk. If I look and listen, not just with my eyes and ears, but with my heart, an image of a new blossom takes shape in my mind—an image that will bloom again for me in fabric.

Kumiko Sudo

Flower Origami: A Guide to Technique

IN THIS BOOK YOU WILL FIND twenty designs that magically transform simple shapes cut from fabric into beautiful decorative flowers. Some of the designs are inspired by my garden and others by the fabrics themselves as my fingers fold them into new shapes. Just as with paper origami, where folds reveal the color and pattern on the reverse side of your paper sheet, the process of combining two fabrics to form three-dimensional flowers surprises and delights with each step.

If you are familiar with my earlier books on creating flowers from fabric, you will immediately see that the designs in *Flower Origami* have a completely different look. In my early flowers, I used a simple soft-fold and stitch technique. Here, the process is a little different. I make firm folds in the fabric, then press to make sure they hold and lie flat. I then make a few stitches to secure the folds. For most designs, I continue by making a new round of folds that reveal the second fabric, just as a flower opens to display new colors and patterns inside the bud. The resulting flowers have an elegant, sophisticated appearance, but are just as quick and easy to make as my earlier designs. I hope they will inspire you to create flowers of your own from simple fabric shapes.

Basic Tool Kit

A list of materials is supplied with every project. In addition, you will need the items listed here. Collect everything you need before you start and keep it all in a box or basket within easy reach. A little preparation will save you time and frustration when you sit down to make a new project.

Hand-sewing needles

Pins and pincushion

High-quality hand-sewing threads in variety of colors

Thimble

Thread snips

Rotary cutter and self-healing cutting mat (optional)

Sharp fabric scissors

Paper scissors

Tailor's chalk, charcoal stick, or other temporary marker

Sharp pencils and eraser

Compass

Ruler

Tracing paper

Template plastic or stiff card

Toothpick or dollmaker's awl

To showcase the flower designs, I have created a quilt block featuring each one. Complete with a special all-in-one border and binding, they make lovely wall-hangings. You may wish to follow the Japanese tradition of changing wall decorations with each season. You will find color schemes and designs in tune with the pleasures of spring, the joy of summer, and the serenity of fall and winter. Try combining two or three completed quilts in the same wall arrangement. The effect can be quite beautiful. Notice, too, that each block is the size of a pillow—it is easy to use the designs for pillow covers that match the quilts. In addition, several of the flower designs are featured on smaller projects, such as elegant evening purses, decorative boxes, sewing kits, and much more. These make wonderful gifts, and they are surprisingly easy to make.

Selecting Fabrics

Before you begin to work with fabrics, look for inspiration in the world around you. Whether you find blossoms on your own garden path, deep in the woods, or in exotic floral arrangements in a flower shop window, each can be recreated in fabric. Look carefully at the colors. A single flower offers an incredible range of hues. Look, too, at the forms of the petals, the buds, and the leaves. These are the shapes you will work with as you mold your fabric into new forms.

Most of the designs in *Flower Origami* are made from contemporary American cottons. Some are from older, Japanese fabrics. To begin making flowers, however, you do not need to start with a large fabric collection. Most of the flowers can be made from quite small scraps, and it is easy to combine several fabrics in the same design. For each project, I have suggested how much fabric you will need, but these quantities are always over generous. A ⅛ yd (15 cm) length, for example, will often allow enough fabric for two or even three flowers. Using the photographs as a guide to contrast (the use of light, medium, and dark tones), I suggest you choose colors and patterns that you enjoy. Lay them out on the background fabric you have selected. Make sure, too, the fabric you have chosen for the border complements the flowers and does not overwhelm them.

Using Templates

There are two types of templates in *Flower Origami*. First, on pages 156 to 159, you will find four full-size templates for the beginning shapes you will use for folding your flowers—a square, a circle, a pentagon, and an octagon. These templates already include ¼" (0.75 cm) seam allowances and—unless you wish to change the size of your flowers—there is no need to adjust them. Second, for each project, full-size appliqué templates are provided for all pieces. *These templates do not include seam allowances.* Sometimes, you will need to draw around these templates to mark a design on your background fabric. When you are ready to cut out your fabric pieces, however, you will need to add a ⅛" (0.4 cm) seam allowance to all appliqué templates, unless indicated otherwise on the template or in the sewing directions. Most of the templates are curved, which means they are easier to cut with very sharp scissors than with rotary cutting equipment. Since the projects are small and multiples of the same pattern piece are rarely needed, hand-cutting is quick and easy. Remember to transfer any markings from the pattern onto the cut pieces of fabric.

Sewing

I sew everything—straight seams and curved seams, piecing and appliqué—by hand. I like the sense of intimacy that hand-sewing gives me. I feel that the hand is directed not only by the eye but by the heart. Since all the flower designs are small, you may want to sew them by hand, too. You'll find that some require only a few stitches. If, however, you prefer to sew by machine, you will find it easy to do so. The circles and squares of back-to-back fabric from

Re-usable Flower Templates

Since many of the flowers are created from the same shapes that you will use over and over again, Flower Origami *is accompanied by a set of durable plastic templates made to the sizes needed to create the flowers in this book. Each one offers a variety of sizes, should you wish to make your flowers smaller than mine. The set includes the following basic beginning shapes—circle, square, pentagon, and octagon. Each already includes ¼" seam allowance and will give you finished shapes measuring:*

Circle: 8", 6" 4½",

Square: 7", 5½", 4"

Octagon: 8", 6½", 5"

Pentagon: 8", 6", 4½"

which most of the flowers are formed are simple to sew by machine. Adding the backing and border is also easy on the machine.

Many of the designs involve sewing curved seams. For perfect curved seams, I use a form of appliqué or invisible stitching that is described below. My technique involves placing a fabric piece, with the seam allowance folded under, on top of a background piece; the piece is then blind-stitched by hand. In the instructions, this is what is meant by the term *appliqué*. The term *sew* indicates a more traditional method of sewing the pieces together, right sides facing, using a running stitch on the wrong side of the seam lines. Straight seams are sewn in this way, and you may use hand or machine stitching.

Invisible Stitches

The appliqué technique I use to attach flowers, leaves, and stems onto the background fabric results in tiny stitches that are not visible from the front of the quilt. The appliqués lie flat, for a smooth, clean effect.

1. Fold under seam allowance of appliqué leaf or stem and finger-press firmly in place. Pin in place through seam allowance onto background fabric. Knot thread, then insert needle through fold line on appliqué fabric (A), at an angle, as shown. Knot will be hidden in folded seam allowance.

2. Insert needle through a single thread in weave of background fabric (B). As soon as it emerges from fabric B, re-insert needle into fabric A at fold line. Exit at a point ¼″ (0.75 cm) further down fold line.

3. Repeat, pulling thread firmly with each stitch. In effect, thread is hidden in "tunnel" inside folded seam allowance of fabric A.

If you are working with slippery fabrics like silks or with small appliqués, it is helpful to baste the seam allowance of the appliqué firmly in place before beginning the invisible stitch. This will

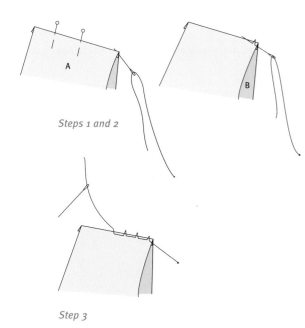

Steps 1 and 2

Step 3

prevent distortion of the fabric. Take care to fold over any tips or sharp corners precisely before basting. Remove basting stitches once the appliqué is in place.

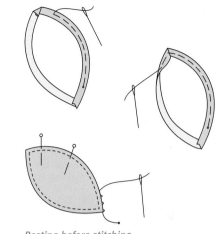

Fabric Origami

All the flower designs in *Flower Origami* are inspired by the Japanese art of origami, or paper folding. Like many Japanese children, I learned the basics of origami at my mother's knee. I loved the colors and patterns in decorative origami papers and would mold them into shapes of my own. Now, instead of paper, I fold fabrics. Even if you know nothing of origami, you will find that my fabric-folding techniques are easy to learn. These tips may help.

Basting before stitching

- Study each folding diagram carefully before you begin. Determine which is the right and wrong side of the fabric. Go through the step-by-step instructions mentally before you even pick up the fabric. You may find it helpful to practice each new shape on a sample so that you solve any difficulties before you begin on your final piece.
- Always fold accurately and neatly.
- Crease each fold firmly with the back of your thumbnail. Good creases make the folding easier, and they serve as guides to future steps.
- One difference between folding paper and folding fabric is that paper is available with different colors on the two sides. To achieve the same effect when folding fabric, you must first sew the two colors of your choice together, then turn them right side out and press. Often, finger pressing will be adequate. Directions for this step are provided on pages 7–8.

You will find that the same procedures are used over and over again. You will soon become so proficient with them that you can carry them out almost without thinking.

Preparing the Background Base for Quilts

All of the blocks in *Flower Origami* are the same size and are constructed in exactly the same way. The complete size, including borders, is 17″ × 17″ (42 cm × 42 cm). The border width is 1½″ (4 cm). To prepare the background base onto which you will appliqué the design, follow these simple steps.

1. Cut square of background fabric measuring 15″ × 15″ (38 cm × 38 cm). This includes ½″ (1.5 cm) seam allowance.
2. Mark seam line ½″ (1.5 cm) inwards from all edges, so that background base onto which you will appliqué measures 14″ × 14″ (35 cm × 35 cm).
3. Carefully and lightly draw complete design onto to background base, using photograph and layout diagram as guides and tracing around templates (make sure you have not yet added seam allowance to templates). Transfer any sashiko design onto base.
4. Center background base on top of batting and baste batting in place. Very thin batting works best and is easier to needle.

You are now ready to appliqué the design of your choice onto the background base.

Adding Sashiko Designs

Rather than use the traditional quilting stitch, I have adapted Japanese sashiko stitching to embellish the quilt blocks in *Flower Origami*. This delicate yet distinctive form of stitching accents the folded flower designs beautifully. The stitching might suggest rays of sunshine, a sudden breeze, or the fluttering wings of a butterfly. Your choice of a contrasting thread color may highlight such effects.

The method of stitching I have used is a combination of the traditional sashiko stitch and the quilting stitch. It is done before the backing and border are completed, so that the stitches do not show through to the back of the quilt.

1. Using stencils provided, lightly mark sashiko design on background base.

2. Without knotting thread, insert needle from front of quilt, at a point about ¼″ (0.75 cm) away from first marked line of sashiko to be completed. Make backstitch to secure thread, then use simple stab stitches to complete design. For each stitch, pull thread through all layers of quilt, exiting on back. Reinsert needle from back to front, taking care to stay on marked design.

3. As you complete design, aim for neat, evenly spaced stitches. You'll find your stitches become smaller with practice. To finish stitching, make another backstitch, then pull needle about ¼″ (0.75 cm) from this point. Clip thread as close to quilt as possible, allowing tail to slip within layers of quilt, where it is hidden from view.

Preparing Flower Shapes

All the origami flower designs begin with a simple shape—a circle, a square, a pentagon, or an octagon. All flower templates already include a ¼″ (0.75 cm) seam allowance. (See page 3 on re-usable templates.) Use the same steps to prepare all shapes, as follows.

1. Using template indicated in pattern you have selected, cut fabrics as needed. Take care to achieve good color contrast between each pair that will be sewn together.

2. Matching contrasting colors (light to dark) and right sides together, sew pairs together by hand or by machine, maintaining even ¼″ (0.75 cm) seam allowance. Leave 2″ (5 cm) opening.

3. Fold both seams inward toward center of shape and press. If you are preparing a circle, follow curved line to make a nice, rounded curve. Turn right side out. For angled shapes, poke a toothpick or dollmaker's awl into angles to assure crisp corners. Blind-stitch opening closed. Lightly press to reinforce shape.

See re-usable templates on page 3

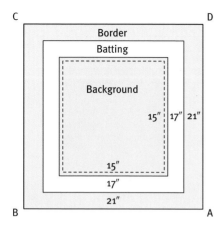

Step 1

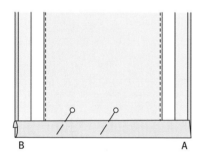

B   A

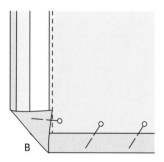

Step 4

Just as in traditional paper origami, which uses paper decorated in different colors and patterns on either side, you now have a two-sided shape to begin folding your flowers.

Adding Backing and Borders

The first step in making each of the small quilts in *Flower Origami* is to prepare the background base onto which you will then appliqué the designs. Unlike traditional quiltmaking, I always baste a layer of thin batting to the background base before I begin the appliqués. Once the design is complete, I add a combined backing/border made from a single piece of fabric. Each finished quilt measures 17″ × 17″ (42 cm × 42 cm), which includes a 1½″ (4 cm) border. I am always careful to choose a beautiful fabric for the backing, since it shows on the border of the quilt. Follow these steps to add the backing and border to the quilt top.

1. Pre-cut background base, batting, and backing/border fabric as follows.

Background base	Batting	Backing/border
15″ × 15″	17″ × 17″	21″ × 21″
(38 cm × 38 cm)	(42 cm × 42 cm)	(52 cm × 52 cm)

2. Wrong sides together, pin quilt top (including batting) to center of backing/border fabric.

3. Fold inwards ½″ (1.5 cm) seam allowances around all sides of backing/border piece.

4. Fold bottom edge (A-B) inward by 1½″ (4 cm) to create bottom border. Folded-in seam allowance aligns with horizontal seam line previously marked on base, ½″ (1.5 cm) in from raw edge. Pin in place. Fold corner B diagonally to meet vertical seam line marked on base. Pin in place.

5. Repeat Step 3, folding top edge (C-D) and corner D.

6. Open out corner C completely (except turned-in seam allowance). Fold left edge (B-C) inwards by 1½″ (4 cm) to create left border. Fold corner C diagonally to meet vertical seam line marked on base. Fold top edge (C-D) inwards by 1½″ (4 cm) to create top border.

7. Repeat Step 4, folding right edge D-A and opening out corner A to create right border.

8. Blind-stitch around all seams, attaching front of border to front of base. There is no need to stitch across diagonals.

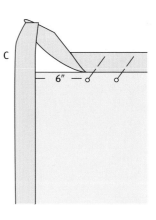

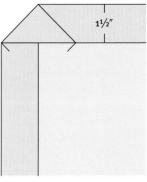

Step 6

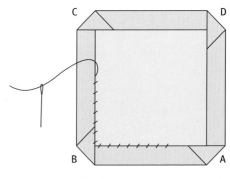

Step 8

目覚め

Awakening

WHEN I WAS VERY YOUNG, my family ran a photo studio in downtown Tokyo. In the evenings, my father would venture out with me into the bustling city streets, crowded with vendors offering all kinds of goods from roadside kiosks. Each was hung with a paper lantern that bathed our faces in the soft red-gold of candlelight as we strolled along. One evening, my tiny rubber shoes stopped in front of a gaming booth, with baby goldfish as prizes. Seeing the gaze of wonder in my eyes, the stall-owner popped a fish into a plastic bag and put it into my little hand. Oh, what joy! Next, we stopped to watch a street merchant prepare cotton candy. First, he poured white crystals of sugar into a shiny metal dish. As he pumped a wooden bar with his foot, a sweet scent floated into the air and, before my eyes, cotton candy rose from the machine in billowing clouds of white and pink. I tried to reach out with my tongue and felt the soft-sweetness touch my face.

Whenever I recall this scene, with my fingers curled inside by father's big hand and the lanterns rocking in a gentle breeze, my mind is filled with ideas for new creations.

"When I try to recall the details of scenes from my past, ideas for new creations rush to mind."

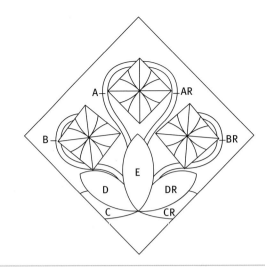

Sun Rose

1. Prepare background base following steps on page 6 and using layout diagram here as a guide. Using ⅛″ (0.4 cm) seam allowance, applique stems A, AR, B, and BR then leaves C, D, and E in place in alphabetical order.

Make three flowers

2. Using circle template X on page 157, cut three from each of two complementary fabrics (one dark, one light). Follow directions on page 7 to prepare circles for folding. Lightly fold circle horizontally then vertically to find center. Mark center lightly on both sides.

3. Fold each side inward by 1″ (2.5 cm) at its midpoint to create a square. Pin in place.

4. Turn over. Fold all corners to center point of square. Make one or two small stitches to secure tip of each corner in place. Press.

Complete

5. See pages 8–9 for directions on adding combined backing/ borders. Position flowers as desired on quilt block and, from underside, make tiny stitches about 1½″ (4 cm) inwards from each corner to hold flowers securely in place.

See templates on page 124.
Add ⅛″ (0.4 cm) seam allowance

MATERIALS YOU WILL NEED

Base: ½ yd (45 cm)

Batting: ½ yd (45 cm)

Backing: ¾ yd (70 cm)

Applique stems and leaves:
   scraps of at least three fabrics

Flower fabrics: ⅛ yd (25 cm) each of
   two fabrics

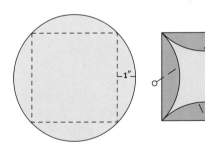

Step 3

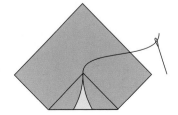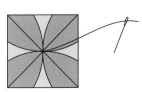

Step 4

Sun Rose *in alternate fabrics*

Sun Rose Sewing Kit

Let this delightful flower box bring the zest of Spring into your home. It makes a lovely sewing kit, prettily accommodating scissors, threads, a thimble, and fabric scraps—there's even a needle case to match! Take the kit along with you to view cherry trees in bloom as you quietly stitch in a shower of falling petals. If you make Sun Rose for someone who doesn't sew, notice that it is the perfect size to neatly disguise a small box of tissues! And you can easily adapt the needle case to fit a small notebook or a few special photographs.

Sewing Box

1. Follow steps 2 to 4 of *Sun Rose* on page 13 to make twelve flowers.
2. Lay out completed flowers in rows of three as shown and in a manner that pleases you. Note that flowers 3, 6, 9, and 12 form bottom of box. As photographed, these flowers are made from the same two fabrics. Pin a number to each flower so that you sew in correct sequence.
3. Pick up flowers 1 and 2. With right sides together, connect along one side using fine coil stitch (see box). In same way, add flower 3. Complete four sets of three flowers.

See template on page 125.
Add ¼" (0.75 cm) seam allowance

MATERIALS YOU WILL NEED

Flower fabrics: ¼ yd (25 cm) each or
   scraps of at least five fabrics

Handles: ⅛ yd (15 cm) or scraps of each
   of two fabrics

12 decorative pearls, beads, or buttons

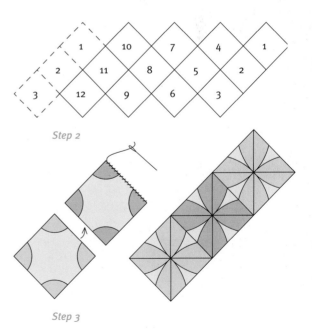

Step 2

Step 3

Coil stitch—begin with backstitch

Work from right to left

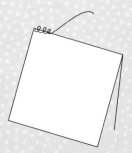

End with backstitches

Coil Stitch

This easy-to-learn technique allows you to connect the flowers together without puckers and with fine, even stitches. Pin two flowers right sides together, aligning the edges. Knot your thread and begin with a double stitch. Taking one stitch at a time and moving from right to left, insert the needle at a 45° angle through the front fabric facing you. Push through all layers and exit the needle at the back of the work, ⅛" (0.4 cm) or less to the left of your entry point. Tug the thread then loop over the top of the work to take your next stitch. When you reach the end of your row of stitches, take three backstitches to secure. The line of stitches on the back side of your work will be on the diagonal; the stitches at the front will be near-invisible and recessed into the fabric.

Diagonal stitches on the back side

Near invisible stitches on the front side

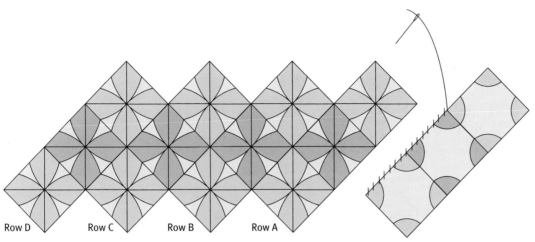

Row D   Row C   Row B   Row A

Step 4

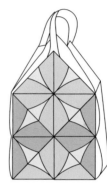

Step 7

4. Using coil stitches and wrong sides together, connect four rows, offsetting each by one flower as shown.

5. To make box bottom, use coil stitch, right sides together, to connect bottom edge of flower 3 in row A to right edge of flower 6 in row B. In same way, sew bottom edge of flower 6 to right edge of flower 9 in row C; sew bottom edge of flower 9 to right edge of flower 12 in row D; sew bottom edge of flower 12 to right edge of flower 3 in row A. The box bottom is magically complete! Turn right side out. If you wish, press lightly to reinforce shape.

6. Stitch decorative bead or pearl to center of each flower, except those on bottom. Stitch another at every point at which four flowers meet, as shown in photograph.

7. Using template F and adding ¼″ (0.75 cm) seam allowance, cut two handle pieces from each of two complementary fabrics. Matching different fabrics and right sides together, stitch around all edges, leaving 2″ (5 cm) opening. Turn right side out and press lightly to reinforce curves at either end. Repeat for second handle. Sew one curved end to wrong side of each of four flower tips at top of box.

8"

3¾"

Center flower is created from 7 tiny
green seed beads and one yellow bead.
Stems of other four flowers are made
from ¼" (0.75 cm) cylindrical beads.

Detail,
beaded flower

Beaded Flowers

Make these tiny flowers from small beads. Sew the center bead to the felt,
exiting the needle on the right side. Using a complimentary color, string
seven beads, allowing them to wrap around the center bead. Draw the
needle back through to the wrong side of the felt, then make two small
stitches at either side of the circle to hold the beads in place. Stitch ¼"
(0.75 cm) cylindrical beads in place to create stems and leaves.

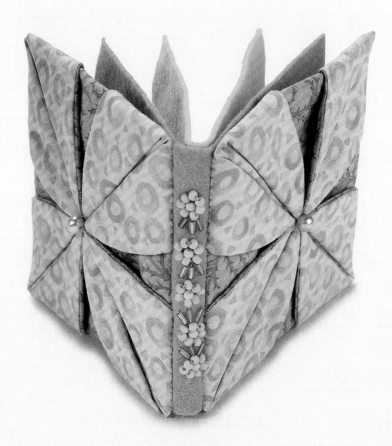

Flower fabrics: ¼ yd (15 cm) or scraps of two fabrics

Felt in two colors: Piece A is 3¾″ × 8″ (9.5 cm x 20 cm); piece B is 3¾″ × 7¾″ (9.5 cm × 19.5 cm)

¼″ (0.75 cm) ribbon: 14″ (35 cm)

2 decorative pearls

Decorative beads to embellish spine

Small thread scissors (optional)

Step 2

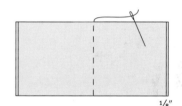

Step 3   ⅛″

Sun Rose Booklet

1. Follow steps 2 to 4 of *Sun Rose* on page 13 to make two flowers.

2. Sew decorative beads as desired or as shown down center of larger piece of felt, piece A.

3. Position smaller piece of felt, piece B, on top of first. Make single line of running stitch down center to hold two pieces together.

4. Position completed flowers on either side of beaded spine. Spine should measure about ½″ (1.5 cm) wide. Pin to hold in place. With felt side facing you, stitch flowers in place along spine edge only.

5. Loop one end of ribbon through one of finger holes in scissors. Fold ribbon over by about ½″ (1.5 cm) and stitch edges to hold scissors securely in place. Fold other end of ribbon over by about 2″ (5 cm) and stitch in place onto felt as shown, leaving ¾″ (2 cm) loop free.

6. If necessary, trim back felt so that it does not show when booklet is closed.

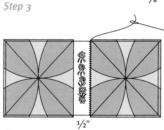

Step 4   ½″

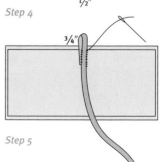

Step 5   ¾″

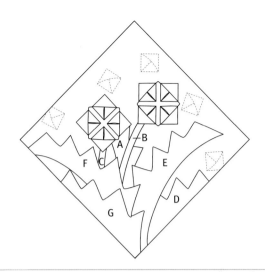

Thistle

1. Prepare the background block following the steps on page 6 and using the layout diagram here as a guide. Using a ⅛″ (0.4 cm) seam allowance, appliqué in place leaf A, stems B and C, then leaves D, E, and F in alphabetical order. Before stitching G in place, trim away extra F fabric that will be covered by G. Lightly mark fabric, then use sashiko or quilting stitches to make sashiko designs. Stitch through background base and attached batting.

Make three flowers

2. Using square template W on page 156, cut three from each of two complementary fabrics (one dark, one light). Follow directions on page 7 to prepare squares for folding. Lightly mark center of square on both sides and add diagonal guidelines on front side only.

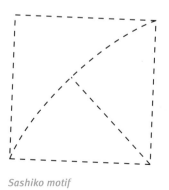

Sashiko motif

See templates on page 125–127.
Add ⅛″ (0.4 cm) seam allowance

MATERIALS YOU WILL NEED

Base: ½ yd (45 cm)

Batting: ½ yd (45 cm)

Backing: ¾ yd (70 cm)

Appliqué stems and leaves: ⅛ yd each
*   of two fabrics plus scraps*
*   of complementary fabrics*

Flower fabrics: ¼ yd (25 cm) each of
*   two fabrics*

A   A

7″

A   A

Step 2

Thistle Tote, *back view*

Thistle Tote

This simple tote is made from rectangles measuring 19" × 15½" (47 cm × 14 cm) backed with fusible interfacing. Lining is cut to 19" × 12½" (47 cm × 31.5 cm). Inside top is finished by a 19" × 4" (47 cm × 10 cm) strip. Flap is made from two 5" × 8" (13 cm × 20 cm) rectangles, and shoulder straps from two 36" × 4" (90 cm × 10 cm) strips. All measurements include ½" (1.5 cm) seam allowance. Although shape of purse is different, construction is similar to Tangerine Tote. Flap is sewn onto back, with a snap fastener or velcro to close at front.

Thistle *in*
alternate fabrics

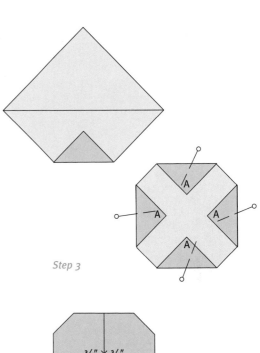

Step 3

3. Fold each corner inwards by about 1¾″ (4.5 cm) along guideline. Press and pin in place.

4. Turn over. Lightly draw a ⅜″ (1 cm) square at very center of piece, using center marking from Step 2 as a guide. Bring each folded corner to center, aligning with new guideline, as shown. You will need to tuck each new fold beneath previous one. Press and pin. Make stitch at each corner of center square through all layers to hold. Notice that you now have a diamond of dark fabric on top of a square of lighter fabric.

5. Open out each corner of light-fabric square completely, pulling point upright. Push down on point, creating triangle of light fabric at corner. Press firmly to hold, then stitch securely at center diagonal, as shown. Add extra stitches to secure each of smaller, dark-fabric triangles at center.

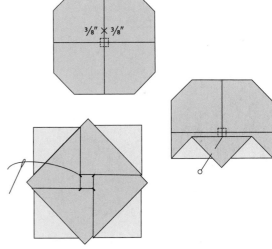

Step 4

Complete

6. See pages 8–9 for directions on adding combined backing/borders. Position flowers as desired on quilt block and, from underside, make tiny stitches close to center to hold securely in place.

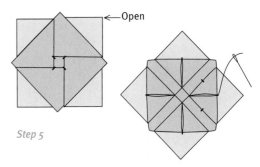

Step 5

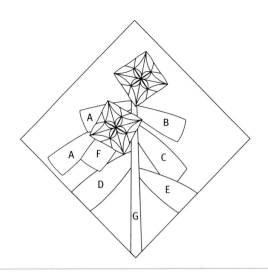

Tangerine

1. Prepare background block following steps on page 6 and using the layout diagram here as a guide. Using ⅛" (0.4 cm) seam allowance, appliqué leaves A to F in alphabetical order. Pin then appliqué stem G to cover inner edges of leaves.

Make two flowers

2. Use circle template X on page 157, cut two from each of two complementary fabrics (one dark, one light). Follow directions on page 7 to prepare circles for folding. Lightly fold circle horizontally then vertically to find center. Mark center lightly on both sides.

3. Fold each side inward by 1" (2.5 cm) at its midpoint to create a square. Press and pin in place. Adjust folds as needed to ensure you have formed neat right angles at each corner of square.

4. Fold same piece back on itself by about ½" (1.5 cm), aligning midpoint with edge of square. Press and pin in place. Make two stitches at each point A, about 1" (2.5 cm) inward from each corner of square. Make sure stitches go through all layers—two folded-over edges and layer behind them. Open out corners by folding back to layer to create petal shape. Press lightly to hold shape.

See template on page 126–127.
Add ⅛" (0.4 cm) seam allowance

MATERIALS YOU WILL NEED

Base: ½ yd (45 cm)

Batting: ½ yd (45 cm)

Backing: ¾ yd (70 cm)

Appliqué stem and leaves: scraps of various complementary fabrics

Flower fabrics: ¼ yd (25 cm) each of two fabrics

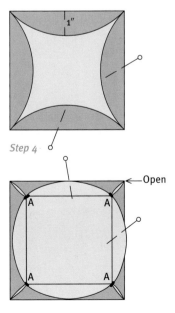

Step 4

Step 5

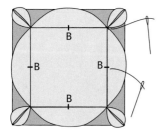

Step 5

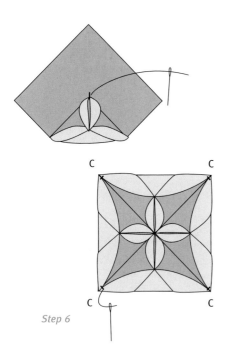

Step 6

5. Make a single stitch at point B, at midpoint of each folded edge.

6. Fold each corner to back as shown, making a single stitch at flower center to hold securely in place. Press. Stitch top layer together at each point C, about ¼″ (0.75 cm) inward from corner. Make another stitch through all layers, exiting needle at back of work.

Complete

7. See pags 8–9 for directions on adding combined backing/borders. Position flowers as desired on quilt block and, from underside, make tiny stitches about 1″ (2.5 cm) inwards from each corner to hold securely in place.

Tangerine *in*
alternate fabrics

Tangerine Tote

It's party time! This elegant, heart-shaped tote is perfect for special occasions. It's also a superb statement of style on casual outings. The pretty triangle of flowers hides a slim pocket, held closed by a simple snap. The flower on the back is one of those special touches that make this hand-made gift so unique.

1. Using small circle template XX on page 157, follow steps 2 to 6 of *Tangerine* on pages 25–26 to make seven flowers.

2. Lay out six flowers as shown. Pick up flowers 1 and 2. With right sides together, connect along one side, using fine coil stitch (see page 16). In same way, add flower 3. Next, join flowers 4 and 5. Use same technique to join row A to row B and row C to row B. Stitch decorative bead or pearl to center of each flower. Add one more bead or pearl at center of the work where four flowers meet.

3. Using complete template H/I and adding ½″ (1.5 cm) seam allowance, cut two from fabric for outer tote. Next, using same fabric, cut two from template H. Using another fabric for lining, cut two from template I. Be sure to add ½″ (1.5 cm) seam allowances around all sides.

4. Position joined flowers onto front of tote, with bottom-most tip of bottom flower lying about ½″ (1.5 cm) from bottom of tote. When positioning flowers, don't forget to allow ½″ (1.5 cm) around entire

See template on page 128.
Add seam allowance as indicated in instructions.

MATERIALS YOU WILL NEED

Outer bag and top lining: ½ yd (45 cm)

Bottom lining: ½ yd (45 cm)

Flower fabrics: ½ yd (45 cm) each of two fabrics

8 decorative beads or pearls

Snap fastener

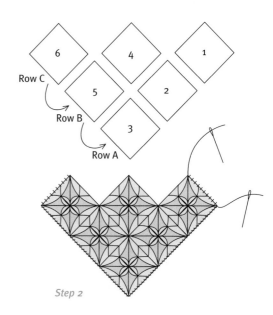

Step 2

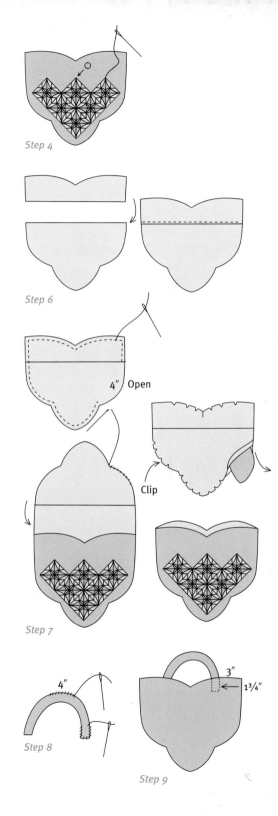

Tangerine Tote,
back view

piece for seam allowance. Stitch joined flowers in place along red line shown here, leaving top open. At tip of center top flower, stitch snap to complete tote pocket. Stitch remaining flower onto back of tote.

5. Right sides together, pin then sew front and back of tote together, leaving top open. Clip curves and press seam allowances to one side to achieve nice, rounded curves. Turn right side out.

6. For lining, turn under bottom seam allowance of piece H and press to stay. Position on top of piece I and pin to hold. Machine or hand stitch together. Repeat with remaining H and I pieces.

7. Right sides together, join front and back lining pieces, leaving about 4″ (10 cm) open as shown. Clip curves and press seam allowances to one side. Do not turn right side out. Wrong sides together, sew top of lining to top of outer bag, stitching around entire circumference. Pull bag through opening in lining. Adjust lining to fit neatly inside outer bag. Blind-stitch opening closed.

8. Using template C and adding ¼″ (0.75 cm) seam allowance, cut four from same fabric as outer tote. Sew two pieces together around all sides, leaving 4″ (10 cm) open at apex of curve. Turn right side out and blind-stitch opening closed. Press to reinforce curved shape. Repeat for second handle.

9. Position handles on inside of tote, as shown. Outer rim of handle should be about 3″ (8 cm) away from center top of tote; about 1¾″ (4.5 cm) of handle should be hidden inside tote. Stitch in place.

Awakening   29

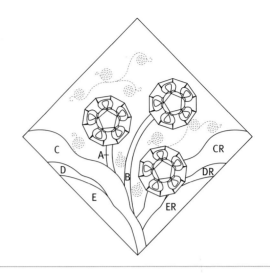

Dwarf Dahlia

1. Prepare background base following steps on page 6 and using layout diagram here as a guide. Using a ⅛″ (0.4 cm) seam allowance, appliqué stems and leaves A to E and AR to ER in place in alphabetical order. Lightly mark fabric, then use sashiko or quilting stitches to make spiral designs. Stitch through background base and attached batting.

Make three flowers

2. Using pentagon template Y on page 158, cut six from each of two complementary fabrics (one dark, one light). Follow directions on page 7 to prepare pentagons for folding.

See template on page 129–130.
Add ⅛″ (0.4 cm) seam allowance

MATERIALS YOU WILL NEED

Base: ½ yd (45 cm)

Batting: ½ yd (45 cm)

Backing: ¾ yd (70 cm)

Appliqué stems and leaves: scraps of at least three fabrics

Flower fabrics: ¼ yd (25 cm) each of two fabrics

Sashiko stitching: three-ply embroidery floss, #25

Sashiko motif

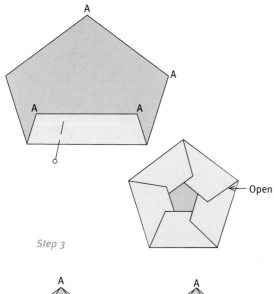

Step 3

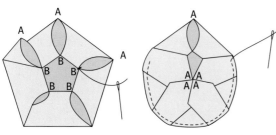

Step 4   *Step 5*

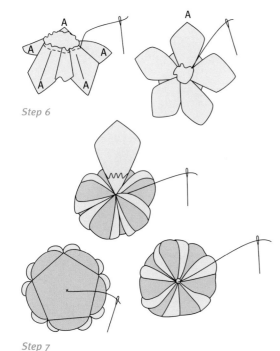

Step 6

Step 7

Make three flower tops

3. Fold each side of a sewn pentagon inward by 1¼″ (3.2 cm), overlapping as shown. When making fifth fold, you will need to undo first one in order to tuck last fold beneath it and to get both to lie correctly. Press and pin in place.

4. Open out each fold of five folds marked in red, pulling tip A of original pentagon toward you. Align edges then make a double stitch at point B. Try to keep sides of small pentagon that forms at center to an even length.

5. Pull tip A toward center of pentagon, flattening each side to create a petal shape, as shown. Pin and press in place. Using strong thread, gather stitch around edges of pentagon, about ¼″ (0.75 cm) in from edge and through all layers.

6. Pull gathering thread firmly, forming circle of about ½″ (1.5 cm) diameter. Remove pins. If your final circle is too big, run second row of gathering stitches over first and pull taut.

7. Fold tips A back toward gathered, stitched center. Stitch once or twice through all layers to hold in place. A small pentagon forms at center on other side of work. As desired, use either side of flower as front.

Dwarf Dahlia *in
alternate fabrics*

Make three flower bottoms

8. Fold each tip A to center of pentagon and stitch in place through all layers.

9. Open out each point B, turning about ⅜″ (1 cm) to back of flower, revealing contrasting fabric and creating petal shape. If desired, stitch to hold at point B.

Complete

10. Position each small flower top on top of large flower bottom. Make one or two small stitches to secure underside of each flower top to center of flower bottom.

11. See pages 8–9 for directions on adding combined backing/borders. Position flowers as desired on quilt block and, from underside, make tiny stitches at two or three points at edges of bottom flowers to secure them to background.

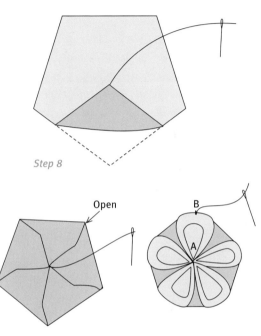

Step 8

Open

B

A

Step 9

Begonia

1. Prepare background base following steps on page 6 and using layout diagram here as a guide. Transfer sashiko design from layout diagram marking it lightly onto background base. Using ⅛″ (0.4 cm) seam allowance, appliqué stems A to D, then leaves E to M in place in alphabetical order. Use embroidery thread in variety of colors to complete sashiko stitching.

Make six flowers

2. Use circle template X on page 157, cut six from each of two complementary fabrics (one dark, one light). Follow directions on page 7 to prepare circles for folding. Lightly mark center of each circle.

3. Fold each side inwards by 1″ (2.5 cm) at its midpoint to create a square. (If you need extra help, lightly draw square onto top fabric before folding.) Press in place. Fold each edge back again by ½″ (1.5 cm) so that apex of curve touches side of newly created square. Pin in place. Stitch once or twice at center to hold. Press.

See template on page 129–133.
Add ⅛″ (0.4 cm) seam allowance

MATERIALS YOU WILL NEED

Base: ½ yd (45 cm)

Batting: ½ yd (45 cm)

Backing: ¾ yd (70 cm)

Appliqué stems and leaves: scraps of at least three fabrics

Flower fabrics: ¼ yd (25 cm) each of two fabrics

Three-ply embroidery floss, #25

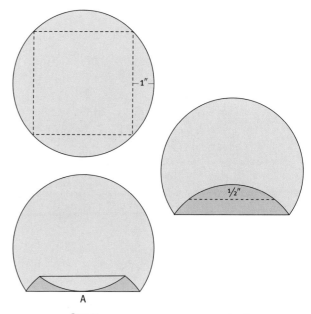

Step 3

Begonia, *sashiko detail*

Fennel Flower, *sashiko detail*

Barberry, *sashiko detail*

Free-Form Sashiko

Similar to the traditional quilting stitch, Japanese sashiko stitching has a rich cultural history. Over time, each region of Japan has developed its own distinct sashiko designs, adding decorative touches to even the plainest of sewing. Rather than follow any particular school, my designs arise from the flowers themselves. I use sashiko to accent my fabric origami designs and to give the block extra dimension. Sometimes, the stitching suggests a falling petal, a spring breeze, or even the whisper of a butterfly as it floats in the air. At other times, the fabric is the inspiration for the design. For Begonia, rather than try to imitate my design precisely, I encourage you to study your own fabric selections and the shapes of your own flowers. My stitching suggests the veins of a leaf; depending upon the colors in your fabrics, your stitching lines may be quite different. Notice, too, that I use a variety of thread colors, allowing all stitching lines to be visible on my multi-colored fabrics. Varying the colors allows you to make some lines prominent while others remain subtle, echoing the patterns of nature.

For Fennel Flower, on page 46, I used the shapes of the appliqué templates to design the sashiko stitching. Simply trace the shapes onto template plastic, then draw around them to mark the design on the fabric. If you wish, vary the size of the shape by about ¼″ (0.75 cm). This effect of mirroring the appliqué shapes gives the impression that the leaves of the flower are swaying gently in an autumn breeze.

Barberry, on page 58, is a most enjoyable method of sashiko. Here, the design is completely free-form. Once a block is finished, I love to study the shapes and then add extra texture by stitching delicate sashiko patterns in open spaces. Sometimes I sketch out the design and trace it onto the fabric. Other times, I let my heart guide my hand as I stitch.

Begonia in alternate fabrics

4. Turn over. Fold all corners to center point of square. Make one or two small stitches to secure tip of each corner in place. Remove pins.

5. Fold each corner inwards by about ¾" (2 cm) and stitch once or twice through all layers to hold.

6. Fold flower in half. Point C is center petal, with B at left and C at right. Fold to insert petal C under petal A and sew. Fold and insert petal B under petal A and sew. Center of back side has only one petal.

Complete

7. See pages 8–9 for directions on adding combined backing/borders. Position flowers as desired on quilt block and, from underside, make tiny stitches at base of each to hold securely in place. If desired, add extra stitch at center top of some or all flowers.

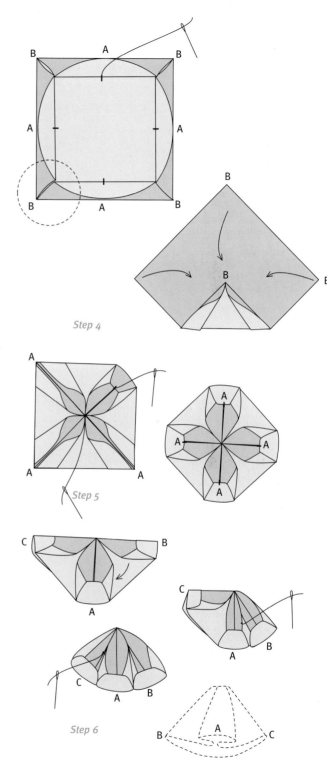

Step 4

Step 5

Step 6

Discovery

I USUALLY SIT AT A WIDE COUNTER in my dining room to
sew. I like this spot because I am surrounded by indoor plants
and can watch the playful world inside the fish tank that sits
on the countertop. One summer evening, I looked up to see
that most of the fish were motionless. More surprising still,
they seemed to have paired themselves off by size and color,
as though lying down to sleep! Just one chubby red gold fish
swam alone at the top of the tank. Next day, I brought home
another red fish. Later that day I was amazed to see the two
of them resting together, side by side. Suddenly inspired,
I rearranged my potted plants into pairs according to color
and variety. I imagined the flowers were thanking me for
their new companions.

Observing the wonders of nature—even those that occur
on my own countertop—helps me understand the interplay of
colors and the balance of design compositions. I am convinced
that every one of my design ideas has its inspiration in the
flowers, the trees, and the little creatures around me.

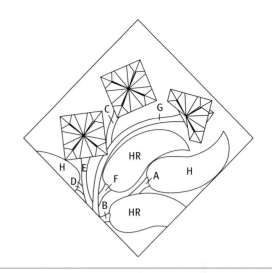

Delphinium

1. Prepare background base following steps on page 6 and using layout diagram here as a guide. Using ⅛″ (0.4 cm) seam allowance, appliqué in place stems A to G, then leaves H and HR. Trim away any excess fabric from H and HR.

Make three flowers

2. Using octagon template Z on page 159, cut three from each of two complementary fabrics (one dark, one light). Follow directions on page 7 to prepare octagons for folding. Lightly draw square as shown as additional guideline. Lightly mark center of square on both sides.

3. Fold four sides inward by about 1″ (2.5 cm) to form square. Press and pin in place.

4. Find point A, at midpoint of each side of small square-within-a-square. Mark at ½″ (1.5 cm) from either side of point A. Make diagonal folds from this point to each corner, as shown. Press and pin.

5. Turn over. Fold each corner to back and stitch to hold at center of flowers. Press firmly.

Complete

6. See pages 8–9 for directions on adding combined backing/borders. Position flowers as desired on quilt block and make tiny stitches close to center of each to hold securely in place. If desired, fold topmost flower in half as shown before attaching to base.

See templates on page 131.
Add ⅛″ (0.4 cm) seam allowance

MATERIALS YOU WILL NEED

Base: ½ yd (45 cm)

Batting: ½ yd (45 cm)

Backing: ¾ yd (70 cm)

Appliqué stems and leaves: ⅛ yd of primary leaf fabric plus scraps of complementary fabrics

Flower fabrics: ¼ yd (25 cm) each of two fabrics

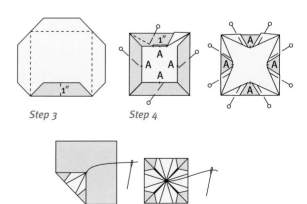

Step 3   Step 4

Step 5

Delphinium Cache

Large enough to hold a driver's license, a lipstick, and a compact, this pretty around-the-neck cache hides any evening's small essentials. Quick to make and charming to wear, it is a perfect hand-made gift for a special friend. You can choose almost any of the flower designs in Flower Origami—Sun Rose *on page 3 is another of my favorites.*

1. Follow steps 2 to 5 of *Delphinium* to make three flowers. Sew decorative pearl or bead to center of each.
2. Fold ribbon end to end, right side out, to make a loop. Sew ends together. Turn wrong side out, and make second row of stitches next to first, hiding raw edges completely. Turn right side out.
3. Fold ribbon in half widthwise along entire length. Position stitched edge at center bottom of first flower. Use overcast stitch to stitch one side of ribbon in place, beginning at center bottom, working around corner and up side seam. Repeat for other side. Do same to attach second flower.

MATERIALS YOU WILL NEED

Flower fabrics: ¼ yd (25 cm) each of two different fabrics

Ribbon for neckband: 2" × 40" (5 cm × 100 cm)

Ribbon for berries: 2" × 10" (5 cm × 25 cm)

Two small pearls or decorative beads

Bulky embroidery thread or thin decorative cord

Scraps of batting

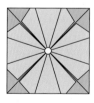

Step 1

Key Fob

Use any of the designs in Flower Origami *to make this pretty key fob. Cut ribbon to desired length. Find center point and wrap ribbon securely around key. Add more keys in same way. Turn under each raw edge of ribbon by about ¼" (0.75 cm) and make single row of running stitch to secure both edges to back of flower.*

Delphinium

4. Leaving lower 3½″ (9 cm) of ribbon open, use small stitches to sew edges of ribbon together.

Make two berries

5. Cut two lengths of ribbon measuring 2″ × 5″ (5 cm x 13 cm). Join seam along longest edge to create tube. Insert knotted length of embroidery thread or thin decorative cord through tube. Gather stitch edge closest to knot and pull thread tightly. Backstitch to hold.

6. Turn right side out, pulling over knot. Stuff with batting. Stitch around loop and pull tight to gather, enclosing knot and batting. Back-stitch to hold. Stitch loose end of embroidery thread or decorative cord to either side of cache, allowing thread to hang about ½″ (1.5 cm) so that berries can swing gently from side to side.

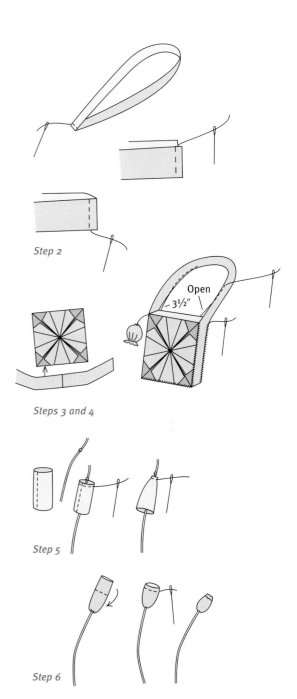

Step 2

Steps 3 and 4

Step 5

Step 6

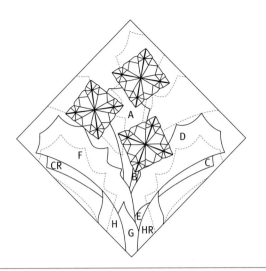

Fennel Flower

1. Prepare background base following steps on page 6 and using layout diagram here as a guide. Using ⅛ ″ (0.4 cm) seam allowance, appliqué in place leaf A, stems B and C, leaf D, stem E and CR, then leaves F, G, H and HR.

2. Transfer sashiko design to base, then use sashiko or quilting stitches to make the nettle shapes. (You can mark around templates A, D, and F to create sashiko design. Do this before adding seam allowance to templates.) Stitch through background base and attached backing. (See page 36 for more help with sashiko stitching.)

Make three flowers

3. Using square template W on page 156, cut three from each of two complementary fabrics (one dark, one light). Follow directions on page 7 to prepare squares for folding. Lightly draw diagonal guidelines on the back and front of fabric square. Mark center.

4. Fold each corner A toward center by 1½″ (4 cm). Press firmly and pin in place.

See templates on page 132–134.
Add ⅛″ (0.4 cm) seam allowance

MATERIALS YOU WILL NEED

Base: ½ yd (45 cm)

Batting: ½ yd (45 cm)

Backing: ¾ yd (70 cm)

Appliqué stems and leaves: scraps of at least four fabrics

Flower fabrics: ¼ yd (25 cm) each of two fabrics

Three-ply embroidery floss, #25

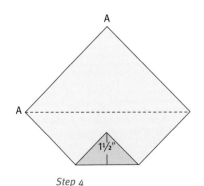

Step 4

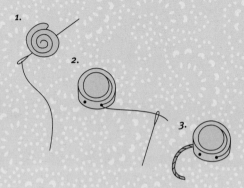

1. Roll felt and stitch to hold
2. Stitch beads in place
3. Add embroidery floss

Back view with business card pocket

Cell Phone Cozy

Cut two pieces of felt measuring 3¾" × 7" (9.5 cm × 18 cm) and two in contrasting color measuring 3½" × 6¾" (9 cm × 17). With sharp scissors, round out tops of all four pieces; cut diagonally across bottoms to create soft V-shape. Cut strips of 1" (2.5 cm) ribbon for stem and leaves. Shape then appliqué in place onto smaller felt shapes. Next, appliqué smaller felt shapes on top of larger ones, then use blanket stitch to sew the cozy together, leaving top open. Stitch two flowers in place around three sides, leaving top open as a pocket. Stitch pearls to center of each flower and along top side of cozy front. Cut three ½" × 2½" (1.5 cm × 6.5 cm) strips of felt in each of two colors and make beads as shown. Stitch one to front of cozy and attach other two with embroidery floss.

Fennel Flower

Fennel Flower *in
alternate fabrics*

5. Fold each side B-B toward center, aligning with corners A as shown to create a square. Press and pin in place, removing pins from A.

6. Turn over. Fold all corners C to center. Press and make one or two stitches at center to hold firmly in place. Remove pins.

7. Fold each side C-D inward, aligning with closest diagonal C-E. A portion of contrast fabric will be revealed. Make one or two stitches through all layers to hold in place.

8. Make a final stitch on underside of each of four center diamonds, at midpoint F. This stitch does not go through top layers of fabric and is completely hidden by folded diamond.

Complete

9. See pages 8–9 for directions on adding combined backing/ borders. Position flowers as desired on quilt block and, from underside, make tiny stitches at center of each to hold securely in place.

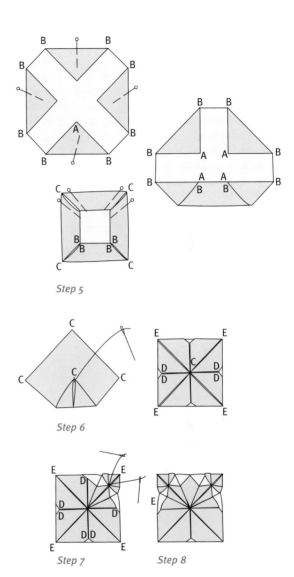

Step 5

Step 6

Step 7   Step 8

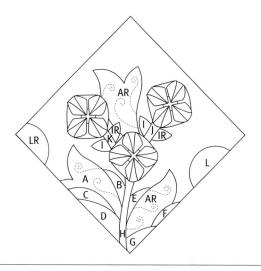

Firewheel

1. Prepare background base following steps on page 6 and using layout diagram here as a guide. Lightly mark sashiko designs as shown on diagram and photograph. Using ⅛″ (0.4 cm) seam allowance, appliqué in place leaf AR at top of block, then leaf B. Appliqué leaf AR to left of block (a portion will overlap into border area). Next, appliqué leaves C and D on top of A. Carefully trim away portions of A hidden under these templates or overlapping into border. In same way, appliqué leaf

See templates on page 135–136. Add ⅛″ (0.4 cm) seam allowance

MATERIALS YOU WILL NEED

Base: ½ yd (45 cm)

Batting: ½ yd (45 cm)

Backing: ¾ yd (70 cm)

Appliqué stems and leaves: scraps of various complementary fabrics

Flower fabrics: ¼ yd (25 cm), each of two fabrics

Three-ply embroidery floss, #25

Sashiko motifs

E and remaining leaf AR to right of block. Appliqué leaves F and G on top or AR, trimming away excess, as before. Complete stem H, leaves I and IR, then stems K and J. Using embroidery thread in one or two colors, stitch sashiko designs as shown.

Make three flowers

2. Using circle template X on page 156, cut three from each of two complementary fabrics (one dark, one light). Follow directions on page 7 to prepare circles for folding.

3. Fold each side inwards by about 1¼″ (3.2 cm) at its midpoint to create square. (If you need to, lightly mark square as shown and fold along guidelines.) Adjust folds as needed to make sure you have formed neat right angles at each corner of square. Press and pin.

4. Turn over. Fold each side of square inwards by 1¼″ (3.2 cm). You will tuck corner of last fold into your first fold. Press, then move pins to hold in place. A small 1″ (2.5 cm) square forms at center.

5. Open out corners to create shape shown. Make double stitch through all layers at point A to hold.

6. Hold tip B upright, then push tip toward but not onto center, creating petal shape. Manipulate with fingers to show more of contrasting fabric. Make a double stitch through all layers at tip and at either side, about ½″ (1.5 cm) from tip.

Complete

7. See pages 8–9 for directions on adding combined backing/borders. Position flowers to cover tops of stems on quilt block and, from underside, make tiny stitches at center of each to hold securely in place.

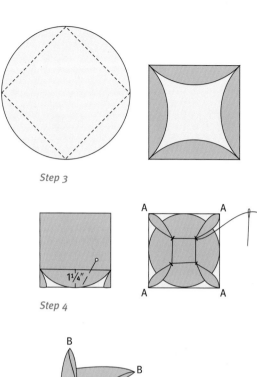

Step 3

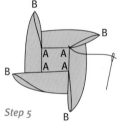

Step 4

Step 5

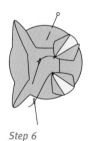

Step 6

Opposite: Use Firewheel *to embellish a simple vest. The hat is decorated with the flower top of* Dwarf Dahlia *(page 30).*

Firewheel Purse

The unique shape makes all the difference! Beautifully designed in worsted cotton for extra durability, Firewheel adds that extra pizzazz to summer evenings. Use it as a clutch purse, as photographed here. If you prefer, it's easy to add a shoulder strap—or even convert it into a head-turner of a backpack. Remember, elegance is in the details—choose your beads and decorative buttons with care.

1. Using circle template X on page 156 but this time adding an extra ¼″ (0.75 cm) all around, follow steps 2 to 6 of *Firewheel* on page 53 to make two flowers. (Either use a compass to draw circle or make new template from template plastic or stiff card.)

2. To make large berries, prepare four pieces of fabric measuring 2½″ × 5½″ (6.5 cm x 14 cm). Follow directions for *Delphinium Cache* on page 45 to complete berries. Make four. Sew about 25 to 30 seed beads to each berry. Use loose end of embroidery thread to attach each berry—one to center of each flower. Save two for back. Allow thread to hang about ½″ (1.5 cm) so that berries swing gently from side to side.

3. Using complete template M/N and adding ½″ (1.5 cm) seam allowance, cut two from fabric for outer bag. Cut two from fusible interfacing. Next, using same fabric, cut two from template M only. Make sure to add ½″ (1.5 cm) seam allowances around all sides.

Templates on pages 137–138. Make complete Template N before cutting fabric. Add seam allowances indicated in steps.

MATERIALS YOU WILL NEED

Outer bag, top lining, and handles:
  ¾ yd (70 cm)

Bottom lining: ½ yd (45 cm)

Fusible interfacing: ½ yd (45 cm)

Flower fabrics: ¼ yd (15 cm) each
  of two fabrics

Berry fabrics: scraps

Leaves: fabric scraps

Decorative buttons: five large, 14 small

Seed beads: approximately 150

Three-ply embroidery floss, #25

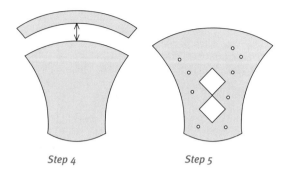

Step 4   *Step 5*

Step 6

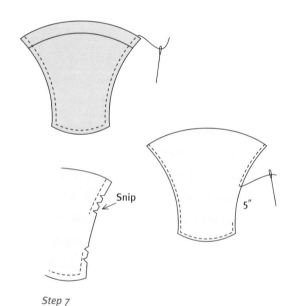

Snip

5″

Step 7

Using another fabric for lining and again adding ½″ (1.5 cm) seam allowance, cut two from template N.

4. With iron, fuse interfacing to each M/N piece for outer bag. Right sides together, stitch one M strip to each M/N piece. Clip seam for nice, smooth curve. Turn right side out and press.

5. Position joined flowers onto one M/N piece for front of purse, with bottom-most tip of bottom flower lying about 2″ (5 cm) from bottom edge of piece. Top-most tip of top flower will fall about 3″ (7.5 cm) from top edge. Make one or two stitches at each corner to sew each flower in place. Sew nine small decorative buttons as desired onto this bag-front piece. Attach remaining two berries and sew four small buttons to purse back.

6. Using leaf template O and adding ¼″ (0.75 cm) seam allowance, cut six from same fabric. Right sides together, sew around pairs by hand or machine, leaving ½″ (1.5 cm) opening. Turn right side out and finger press. Blind-stitch opening closed. Make three. Attach as desired to other M/N piece for back of bag. Use line of stitching that imitates veins on leaf, stringing about seven seed beads per leaf as you sew.

7. Right sides together, stitch around all outside edges of M/N pieces as shown, leaving top open. Repeat with lining pieces N, but leave about 5″ (13 cm) open as shown. Snip seam allowance to achieve smooth curves.

8. With right side of lining and right side of strip M facing toward you, slip lining beneath M strip and pin to hold. Stitch by hand or by machine around entire piece, so that lining is held securely inside purse. Turn right side out, then blind-stitch opening closed. Position lining snugly inside purse.

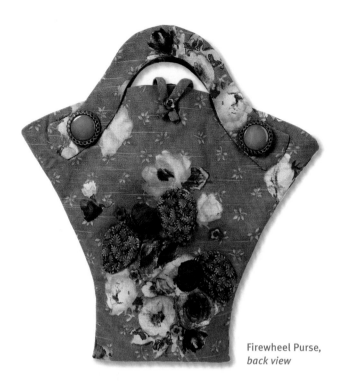

Firewheel Purse,
back view

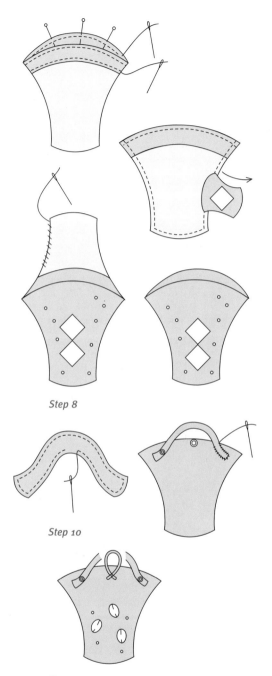

Step 8

Step 10

Step 11

9. Using handle template P and adding ¼″ (0.75 cm) seam allowance, cut four from same fabric as outer purse and two from fusible interfacing. With iron, fuse interfacing to two P fabrics. Match one piece with interfacing to one without and sew them together around all sides, leaving 2″ (5 cm) open along one side. Turn right side out and blind-stitch opening closed. Press to reinforce curved shape. Repeat for second handle.

10. Position handles on outer purse. Use fine overcast stitch as shown to attach. Sew three large buttons to front and two to back.

11. Cut strip of fabric measuring 1½″ × 4″ (4 cm × 10 cm). Fold in half lengthwise, then stitch to make tube. Turn in, then overcast stitch raw edges. Attach as shown to back of purse to make button loop. Add small button to hide stitches.

Barberry

1. Prepare background base following steps on page 6 and using layout diagram here as a guide. Lightly mark as much as you can of the sashiko design onto base. Using ⅛″ (0.4 cm) seam allowance, appliqué leaves A to F, then stems G to I in place in alphabetical order. Using embroidery thread in one or two colors, stitch the sashiko design. (See page 36 for more help with sashiko stitching.)

Make three flowers

2. Using octagon template Z on page 159, cut three from each of two complementary fabrics (one dark, one light). Follow directions on page 7 to prepare octagons for folding.

3. Lightly draw square as shown onto one side of flower piece. Fold each side inwards by 1″ (2.5 cm) along guideline to create perfect square. Press and pin.

See templates on page 135–138.
Add ⅛″ (0.4 cm) seam allowance

MATERIALS YOU WILL NEED

Base: ½ yd (45 cm)

Batting: ½ yd (45 cm)

Backing: ¾ yd (70 cm)

Appliqué leaves: scraps of at least three fabrics

Flower fabrics: ¼ yd (25 cm), each of at least two fabrics

Three-ply embroidery floss, #25

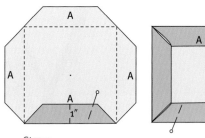

Step 3

Barberry *in*
alternate fabrics

4. Turn over. Fold each corner of square to center, making smaller square shape. Stitch once or twice to hold.

5. Fold each corner of new square inwards by about 1″ (2.5 cm) and stitch to hold.

6. Fold back top layer only of folded corner by about ½″ (1.5 cm), revealing contrasting fabric. Stitch to hold. Repeat on all four sides. Press.

Complete

7. See page 8–9 for directions on adding combined backing/borders. Position flowers as desired on quilt block and, from underside, make tiny stitches at center of each to hold securely in place.

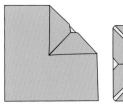

Step 4

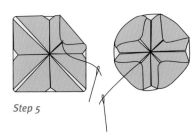

Step 5

Step 6

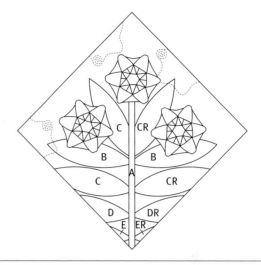

Gloriosa Daisy

1. Prepare background base following steps on page 6 and using layout diagram here as a guide. Lightly mark as much as you can of sashiko design onto base. Cut strip of fabric measuring ¾″ × 14″ (2 cm × 35 cm) for stem A. Using ⅛″ (0.4 cm) seam allowance, appliqué stem A, then leaves B to E and CR to ER in place in alphabetical order. Mark rest of the sashiko design where it overlaps leaves. Using embroidery thread, stitch sashiko design.

See templates on page 139.
Add ⅛″ (0.4 cm) seam allowance

MATERIALS YOU WILL NEED

Base: ½ yd (45 cm)

Batting: ½ yd (45 cm)

Backing: ¾ yd (70 cm)

Appliqué leaves and stems: scraps of three different fabrics

Flower fabrics: ¼ yd (25 cm) each of at least two fabrics

Three-ply embroidery floss, #25

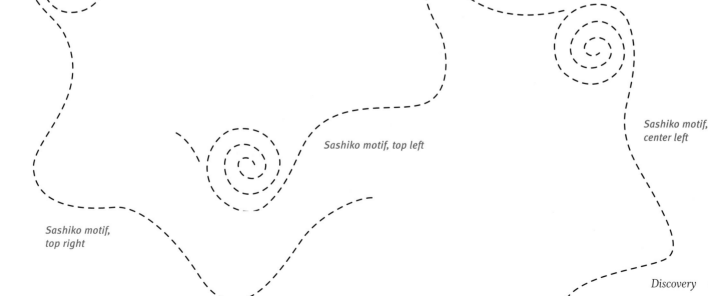

Sashiko motif, center left

Sashiko motif, top left

Sashiko motif, top right

Making Hydrangea

1. Prepare square template Y as on page 157. Lightly mark ¼" (0.75 cm) square at very center on both sides. Fold in corners toward center, until tips touch sides of marked square.

2. Pin then stitch tips in place. Press. Turn over. Again fold in tips to touch center square, then pin, stitch, and press.

3. Reach to back and pull single layer of tip from center, pulling all the way over corner to front, reversing fabric. Repeat at other corners. Stitch in place at center square on front.

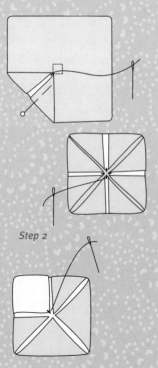

Step 2

Step 3

Lavender Sachet

Bursting with the sweet scent of lavender, every home has a place for this delicate pillow. Cut two 8" (20 cm) circles from velvet. Right sides together, sew around perimeter, leave a 2½" (6.5 cm) opening. Turn right side out, stuff with dried lavender, and blind-stitch opening closed. With strong thread, sew flower to center, bringing thread all way through to back of pillow. Add button and ribbon tassels to embellish.

Gloriosa Daisy *in alternate fabrics*

Make three flowers

2. Using circle template X on page 157, cut three from each of two complementary fabrics (one dark, one light). Follow the directions on page 7 to prepare circles for folding. Use hexagon template V on page 160 to lightly draw a hexagon at the center of one side of each flower piece.

3. Fold curved edges of circle inward along hexagon guidelines marked, forming smaller hexagon of about 1″ (2.5 cm) diameter at center. You will need to tuck last fold beneath first fold. Press firmly and pin to hold.

4. Pull first fold upright at fold line, as shown. Where these two layers meet at edge of small center hexagon, make one or two stitches to secure to each other and to base. Next, open out then push fold back down to reveal portion of contrasting fabric. Stitch at center to hold.

5. Fold about ⅜″ (1 cm) of fabric between each hexagon point to back of piece, stitching in place at back. This slightly curved fold creates star shape of final flower.

Complete

6. See pages 8–9 for directions on combined backing/borders. Position flowers as desired on quilt block and, from underside, make tiny stitches near center of each to hold securely in place.

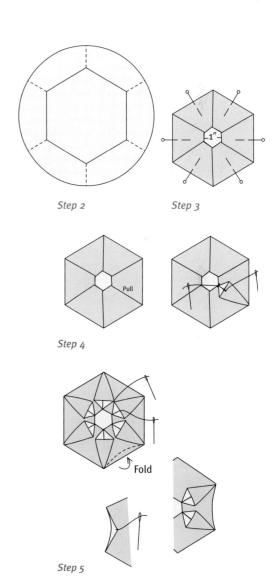

Step 2   Step 3

Step 4

Step 5

Joy

I LOVE TO LOOK AT MAGAZINES on home design and decoration. Often, the pages fall open at beautiful photographs of sparse rooms, painted in shades of white, with a single, perfect focal point. Sometimes I think I would like such a peaceful, organized space in my own home . . . but I quickly reconsider. Every room in my house is populated by decorative crafts. I am particularly fond of dolls and stuffed animals. Some have lived with me a very long time, others are new. As I enter a room, I imagine that I have interrupted their play and can almost hear the dolls whisper to me. New ideas for designs and for stories often come to me while I visit my little friends. Like a child, I dress up a doll in a bright red outfit and see her eyes shine and her lips move into a smile. My heart and hers fill with happiness, as I begin to see the world through her eyes. The same feelings come when I visit the flowers in my garden. I gently touch their petals and speak softly to them. They reward me with lengthier, prettier bloom. No white rooms, no matter how sophisticated the design, can replace the comfort and companionship of my home.

"Seeing the world through the eyes of others is a deep and rewarding source of inspiration."

Star Allium

1. Prepare background base following steps on page 6 and using layout diagram here as a guide. Using ⅛" (0.4 cm) seam allowance, appliqué leaves and stems A to P in place in alphabetical order.

Make three flowers

2. Using circle template X on page 156, cut three from each of two complementary fabrics (one dark, one light). Follow directions on page 7 to prepare circles for folding.

3. Fold each side inwards by about 1⅛" (3 cm) at its midpoint to create square. (If you wish, mark guidelines lightly as shown or just imagine square drawn at center of circle and press in place.) Adjust folds as needed to ensure you have formed neat right angles at each corner. Press and pin in place.

4. Turn over. Fold each corner to center to create new, smaller square. Again, manipulate with fingers to make sure corners are

See templates on pages 140–142.
Add ⅛" (0.4 cm) seam allowance

MATERIALS YOU WILL NEED

Base: ½ yd (45 cm)

Batting: ½ yd (45 cm)

Backing: ¾ yd (70 cm)

Appliqué leaves and stems: ¼ yd (25 cm) each of at least four fabrics

Flower fabrics: ¼ yd (25 cm) each of at least two fabrics

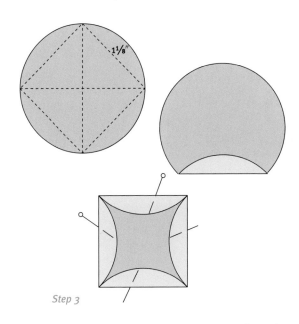

Step 3

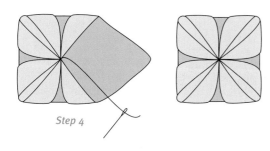

Step 4

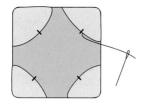

Step 5

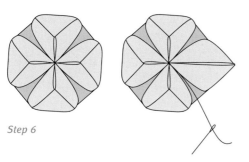

Step 6

sharp. If necessary, make single stitch at very tip of each corner to reinforce sharp point. Press and reposition pins to hold.

5. Turn over to flower back and make double stitch through all layers to hold curved pieces at corners in place.

6. Turn over to flower front. Turn each corner of square inwards by about ½″ (1.5 cm). Make double stitch at tip and through all layers to hold in place. Notice that final flower now has soft, circular shape.

Complete

7. See pages 8–9 for directions on adding combined backing/ borders. Position flowers as desired on quilt block and make tiny stitches close to center of each to hold securely in place.

Star Allium Pochette

Easy to make from simple fabric squares and a strip of ribbon, this pretty little clutch purse adds a touch of chic, no matter how casual the occasion. Or replace the fabric lining with a waterproof one—and transform Star Allium *into a pretty cosmetics tote.*

1. Using small circle template XX and just two fabrics, follow steps 2 to 7 of *Star Allium* on page 00 to make three flowers. Sew decorative pearl to center of each. Place three flowers in row, then use coil stitch (see page 00) to connect them as shown. Outer petals are connected by about ¼″ (0.75 cm) of stitching. Set aside.

2. Cut two 10½″ (27 cm) squares of lining fabric. Right sides together and using generous 1″ (2.5 cm) seam allowance, take running stitch along two opposite edges. Use a ½″ (1.5 cm) seam allowance to sew bottom edge. Fold top edge downwards by 1½″ (4 cm).

MATERIALS YOU WILL NEED

Purse fabric: ½ yd (45 cm)

Lining fabric (waterproof material optional): ½ yd (45 cm)

Flower fabrics: ½ yd (45 cm) each of two different fabrics

Ribbon (or use length of lining fabric): 1½″ × 20″ (4 cm × 50 cm)

Six small pearls or decorative beads

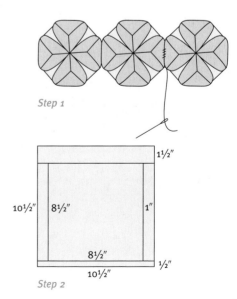

Step 1

Step 2

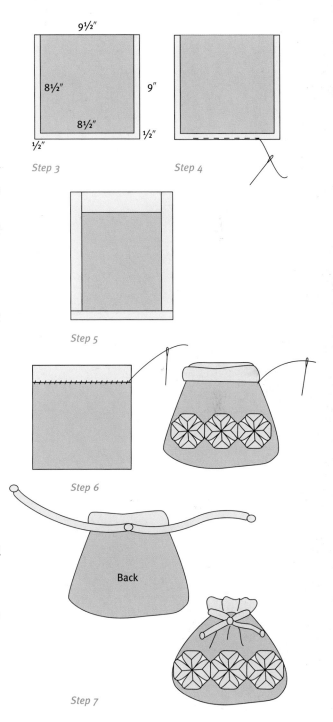

Step 3

Step 4

Step 5

Step 6

Step 7

Back

3. Cut two pieces measuring 9½″ × 9″ (24 cm x 23 cm) for outer bag. Right sides together and using ½″ (1.5 cm) seam allowance, take running stitch along shorter sides and bottom.

4. Leaving both bags wrong sides out, position outer purse on top of lining piece. Use running stitch to sew through all layers inside bottom seam allowance as shown.

5. Press all seam allowances inward as shown, so that all allowances from lining overlap those of outer bag. Press in place then turn outer bag right side out.

6. Fold top edge of outer bag downwards by ½″ (1.5 cm) then again by 1″ (4 cm). Hem, using small stitches. When finished, fold top edge down by another 1″ (2.5 cm), hiding stitches. Make small stitch at right and left seams to hold in place. Attach row of flowers from step 1 by making small stitches through all layers at center of each flower.

7. Fold length of ribbon or lining fabric in half lengthwise and sew long edge, leaving 2″ (5 cm) opening at center. Turn right side out. Blind-stitch opening closed. Turn each end inward by about ½″ (1.5 cm), then gather stitch around circumference. Pull gathers taut, then string pearl or decorative bead onto needle. Stitch pearl or bead in place. Stitch a third bead to center of ribbon, continuing your stitch through tie and through back center of purse, exactly where folded-back lining meets outer purse. Make a second stitch to secure ribbon in place. Tie ribbon at front of purse. Push bottom corners of purse inward by about 1″ (2.5 cm), allowing it to stand.

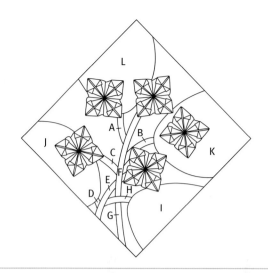

Mallow Rose

1. Prepare background base following steps on page 6 and using layout diagram here as a guide. Using ⅛″ (0.4 cm) seam allowance, appliqué in place stems A to H, then leaves I to L in alphabetical order.

Make five flowers

2. Using square template W on page 156, cut five from each of two complementary fabrics (one dark, one light). Follow directions on page 7 to prepare squares for folding. Lightly mark center of square on both sides and add diagonal guidelines on front side only.

3. Fold each corner inward by about 1½″ (4 cm) along guideline. Press and pin in place. Remove pin, then fold over again by about ⅞″ (2.2 cm). Press and pin. You should have a perfect square.

See templates on pages 142–143.
Add ⅛″ (0.4 cm) seam allowance

MATERIALS YOU WILL NEED

Base: ½ yd (45 cm)

Batting: ½ yd (45 cm)

Backing: ¾ yd (70 cm)

Appliqué stems and leaves: ⅛ yd of primary leaf fabric plus scraps of complementary fabrics

Flower fabrics: ¼ yd (25 cm) each of two fabrics

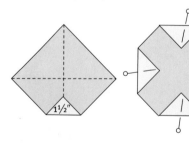

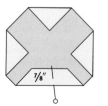

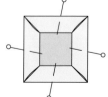

Step 3

Embellished Pillow

Buy or make a rounded pillow measuring about 6" × 15" (15 cm × 38 cm). Make outer casing from 21" × 36" (52 cm × 90 cm) rectangle of plush velvet. Sew longer sides together to make tube; turn right side out. Make 2" (5 cm) hem at ends. Insert pillow. Gather stitch next to pillow and pull taut. Stitch to hold, encasing pillow. Tie decorative ribbon in place. Attach flowers, stitching extra ribbon to center, as desired; Hydrangea (see page 64) is shown here.

Mallow Rose *in alternate fabrics*

4. Turn over. Fold each corner to center and stitch to hold. Fold each side A-B inwards, aligning with the closest diagonal A-C. A portion of contrast fabric will be revealed. Make one or two stitches through all layers to hold in place.

5. Make a ¼″ (0.75 cm) tuck at midpoint of each side to give flowers extra dimension.

Complete

6. See pages 8–9 for directions on adding combined backing/borders. Position flowers as desired on quilt block and make tiny stitches at corners to hold securely in place.

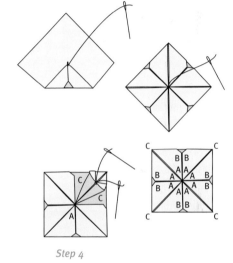

Step 4

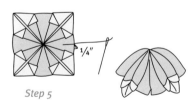

Step 5

Dwarf Primrose

1. Prepare background base following steps on page 6 and using layout diagram here as a guide. Using ⅛″ (0.4 cm) seam allowance, appliqué stems A to C, then leaves D and E in place in alphabetical order.

Make three flowers

2. Using circle template X on page 156, cut three from each of two complementary fabrics (one dark, one light). Follow directions on page 7 to prepare circles for folding. Lightly mark center of each circle, then mark across center, horizontally and vertically.

3. Starting at left side of circle, fold curved edge inward toward center. Press then stitch once or twice at center to hold. Repeat with top edge and right edge. Next fold bottom edge; you will need to open out bottom left corner and tuck fabric beneath first fold. Again, stitch at center to hold. Press. You should now have a perfect square.

See templates on page 144–145.
Add ⅛″ (0.4 cm) seam allowance

MATERIALS YOU WILL NEED

Base: ½ yd (45 cm)

Batting: ½ yd (45 cm)

Backing: ¾ yd (70 cm)

Appliqué stems and leaves: ¼ yd
   (25 cm) decorative floral fabric for
   leaves; scraps for stems

Flower fabrics: ¼ yd (25 cm) each of
   two fabrics

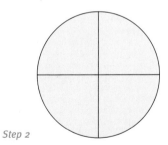

Step 2

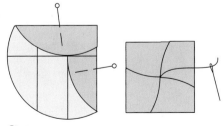

Step 3

Gift Wrapping

Origami flowers are a beautiful way to wrap a gift—the embellishment is so unique that it is cherished as much as the present hidden inside the box. Choose a ribbon in a color that complements your fabrics, tape it in place, and disguise the tape with the flower.

Fennel Flower

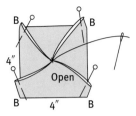

4. Open out each corner fully, pulling fabric upright. Remove pins. Push sides down again, revealing contrast fabric. Top and bottom layers at corners should align perfectly. Pin to hold.

5. Fold back curved edge by about ⅜″ (1 cm), revealing more of contrast fabric and creating petal shape. Make one or two secure stitches through all layers. Remove pins. Manipulate fabric to achieve petal shape shown.

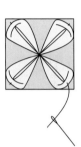

Step 5

Complete

6. See pages 8–9 for directions on combined backing/borders. Position flowers as desired on quilt block and, from beneath, make tiny stitches about 2″ (5 cm) inwards from corner of each to hold securely in place.

Dwarf Primrose *in alternate fabrics*

Dwarf Primrose Tote

Reflecting the shades of summer, this elegant purse adds extra sparkle to casual outings or an air of glamor to evenings out on the town. As shown here, the fabric used for the insides of the flowers has a light shimmer. I chose five tones of the same fabric for a subtle yet colorful effect.

1. Using small circle template XX on page 156, cut 11 from one fabric (in photograph, side-panel fabric is used for all flowers), then 11 more from selection of three or more similar fabrics (I chose five tones of same fabric). Follow steps 2 to 4 of *Dwarf Primrose* on pages 80–81 to make 11 flowers. For three flowers, follow step 5 to reveal more of inside fabric; for remaining flowers, make a stitch at center of each petal, as shown.

2. Cut two squares of fabric measuring 10½″ × 10½″ (27 cm × 27 cm) for purse front and back and two strips of complementary fabric measuring 3″ × 10½″ (7.5 cm × 27 cm) for side panels. All

MATERIALS YOU WILL NEED

Outer bag: ½ yd (50 cm) each of two fabrics (one for front/back; one for side panels)

Inner lining: ½ yd (45 cm)

Flower fabrics: ¼ yd (30 cm) each of at least two fabrics

25 decorative beads or pearls

¾″ (2 cm) button

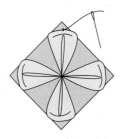

Step 1

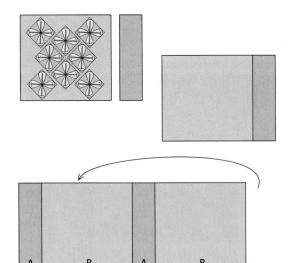

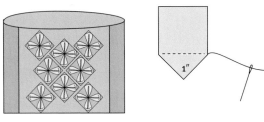

Step 2

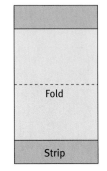

Step 4

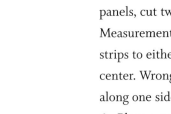

Step 5

measurements include ½″ (1.5 cm) seam allowance. Right sides together, sew a side strip to each larger piece. Join in ABAB sequence shown. *Option:* If you would like your purse to have a softer, fuller look, attach thin batting to one or both purse fabrics before sewing.

3. Attaching beads and stitching only once or twice at center of each, sew eight flowers to front and three to back, as photographed. Attach seven beads to each side panel.

4. Wrong side out, sew side seams then bottom seam. About 1″ (2.5 cm) inwards from each bottom corner, sew a seam diagonally across corner.

5. From lining fabric, cut rectangle of lining fabric measuring 12½″ × 19″ (31.5 cm × 47 cm). From same fabric used for side-panels, cut two strips measuring 3″ × 12½″ (7.5 cm × 31.5 cm). Measurements already include ½″ (1.5 cm) seam allowance. Sew strips to either end of rectangle as shown, then fold and press across center. Wrong sides together, sew sides, leaving a 6″ (15 cm) opening along one side.

6. Place outer purse inside lining pouch. Sew top seams. Pull bag through opening in lining. Blind-stitch opening closed.

7. Cut two strips of purse fabric measuring 4″ × 13″ (10 cm × 32 cm). Turn in long edges by ¼″ (0.75 cm) and press. Fold one long edge to center and stitch in place. Repeat with other long edge. Cut a strip of side-panel fabric measuring 1¾″ × 14″ (4.5 cm × 34 cm). Turn in long edges by ¼″ (0.75 cm), then fold in three, widthwise.

Dwarf Primose Tote,
back view

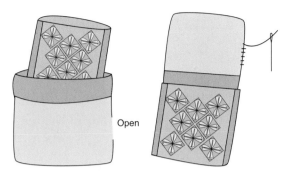

Open

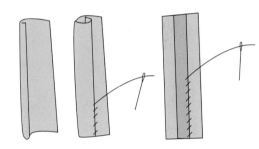

Use tiny hem stitches to stitch in place along center of first strip, hiding previous rows of stitches.

8. Position ends of completed handle on inside of purse and hem stitch in place so that 1½″ (4 cm) remains inside. Sew button at center front of purse, about ½″ (1.5 cm) from top.

9. Prepare strip of side-panel fabric measuring 1″ × 10″ (2.5 cm × 25 cm). Turn in short edges by ¼″ (0.75 cm) and press. Sew long edges together and turn right side out. Attach a decorative bead to each end to close. Make neat knot about 1″ (2.5 cm) Stitch around entire knot to attach strip to center back of purse, about ½″ (1.5 cm) from top.

Step 8

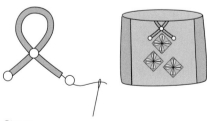

Step 9

Wild Poppy

1. Prepare background block following steps on page 6 and using layout diagram as a guide. Using ⅛″ (0.4 cm) seam allowance, appliqué stems A to C, then leaves D to J in alphabetical order. Lightly mark sashiko designs onto base. Stitch using embroidery thread through base and attached batting.

Make three flowers

2. Using octagon template Z on page 159, cut three from each of two complementary fabrics (one dark, one light). Follow directions on page 7 to prepare octagons for folding. Lightly mark center of octagon on both sides and add guidelines on front side only from top to bottom and side to side as shown. Draw another set of guidelines 1½″ (4 cm) inward from each point A.

See templates on page 145–146. Add ⅛″ (0.4 cm) seam allowance

MATERIALS YOU WILL NEED

Base: ½ yd (45 cm)

Batting: ½ yd (45 cm)

Backing: ¾ yd (70 cm)

Appliqué stems and leaves: ⅛ yd of primary leaf fabric plus scraps of complementary fabrics

Flower fabrics: ¼ yd (25 cm), each of two fabrics

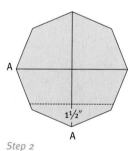

Step 2

Sashiko motif, reverse for one

Wild Poppy in alternate fabrics

3. Fold each point A inwards by about 1½″ (4 cm) along guideline. Press and pin in place. You will need to undo first fold and tuck last fold beneath it. You should now have a perfect square, with a four-pointed star in middle.

4. Turn over. Fold all corners to center and stitch once or twice to hold. Press, making sure all corners are sharp.

5. Pull out then flatten down point B to create a small triangle at center of flower and reveal more of contrast fabric. Stitch in place through all layers.

6. Fold corners inward toward center, stopping at outer edge of small inner triangles. Stitch at tip. Manipulate fabric to form petals as in photograph. Press flower firmly.

Complete

7. See pages 8–9 for directions on adding combined backing/borders. Position flowers as desired on quilt block and make tiny stitches close to center to hold securely in place.

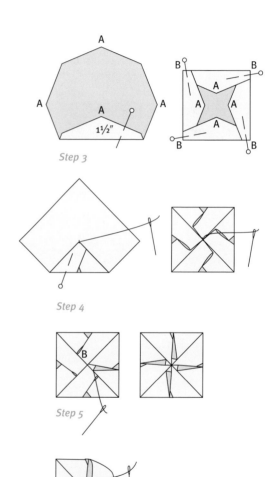

Step 3

Step 4

Step 5

Step 6

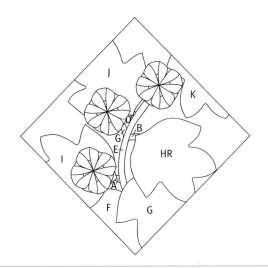

Tulip Tree

1. Prepare background base following steps on page 6 and using layout diagram here as a guide. Using ⅛" (0.4 cm) seam allowance, appliqué stems A to E, then leaves F to K in place in alphabetical order.

Make three flowers

2. Using circle template X on page 157, cut three from each of two complementary fabrics (one dark, one light). Follow the directions on page 7 to prepare circles for folding. Mark center of circle. Position small octagon template ZZ on page 159 at center of circle and lightly mark around it. Repeat on other side of fabric circle.

3. Fold each point A to center and press firmly. You will need to undo first fold in order to tuck last fold beneath. You should have a perfect square. Stitch each point A once or twice at center to hold. Open out each corner fully, pulling petals upright.

See templates on pages 147–146.
Add ⅛" (0.4 cm) seam allowance

MATERIALS YOU WILL NEED

Base: ½ yd (45 cm)

Batting: ½ yd (45 cm)

Backing: ¾ yd (70 cm)

Appliqué leaves and stems: ¼ yd (25 cm) of main leaf fabric, plus scraps of two others

Flower fabrics: ¼ yd (25 cm) each of at least two fabrics

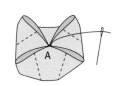

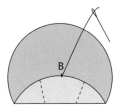

Step 2

Step 3

Scarf Clasp

Soft and textured, fabric flowers make a simple yet elegant fashion statement. Use a safety pin to attach a flower to a scarf, as shown here. Or pin one to a favorite jacket or sweater. For a very special occasion, attach a wristband and transform a fabric flower into a prom-night corsage.

Tulip Tree

Tulip Tree *in
alternate fabrics*

4. Push each corner inward, creating new fold along original octagon guideline. Press to hold. Note that original octagon shape is recreated. Make stitch about ⅜″ (1 cm) away from base at each point of octagon. Make sure needle goes through base as well as both sides of fold.

5. Make ½″ (1.5 cm) tuck in base of each petal and, from back, stitch to hold.

6. Fold petal fabric back by about ½″ (1.5 cm) to reveal contrasting fabric.

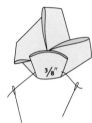

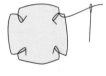

Step 4

Complete

7. See pages 8–9 for directions on adding combined backing/ borders. Position flowers as desired on quilt block and make tiny stitches at two opposite corners of each to hold securely in place.

Tuck

Step 5

"Intuition is cultivated
over time, fueled
by sensations
and experiences."

Serenity

PEOPLE OFTEN ASK HOW I AM ABLE to quickly choose combinations of colors and fabrics that almost instantly meld into balanced designs. The only answer I am able to offer is that my color sense is intuitive. As unreasonable as this at first sounds, I try to explain intuition as a sense that is cultivated over a long period of time through a variety of incidents or experiences. It blossoms in my mind, year after year, and is expressed through my hands.

Observing the changing of the seasons helps develop my intuition. From my living room window I watch the changing colors of a mountain landscape reflected in the waters of a lake. In spring and early summer, my heart rejoices at the beauty of fresh green. Slowly comes the melody of autumnal tints, then the deep grays of winter. A summer sunset, first light pinks and purples, turns to dark orange then to blazing red within minutes. Soon, all that remains is a slender line of red across the horizon. Through the filter of my mind, each blending of colors I see softens or brightens until it finds its way into my work through fabric.

Compositae

1. Prepare background base following steps on page 6 and using layout diagram here as a guide. Using a ⅛″ (0.4 cm) seam allowance, appliqué leaves A and AR, stems B, CR, and C, then leaves D to G in place in alphabetical order.

Make three flowers

2. Using circle template X on page 157, cut three from each of two complementary fabrics (one dark, one light). Follow the directions on page 7 to prepare circles for folding.

3. Fold each side inwards by about 1″ (2.5 cm) at its midpoint and press. (If you wish, mark guidelines lightly as shown or just imagine a square drawn at center of circle and press in place.) Fold back again by about ½″ (1.5 cm) as shown. Pin and stitch at midpoint to hold. You should have a perfect square.

See templates on pages 149–150. Add ⅛″ (0.4 cm) seam allowance

MATERIALS YOU WILL NEED

Base: ½ yd (45 cm)

Batting: ½ yd (45 cm)

Backing: ¾ yd (70 cm)

Appliqué leaves and stems: ¼ yd (25 cm) each of at least four fabrics

Flower fabrics: ¼ yd (25 cm), each of at least two fabrics

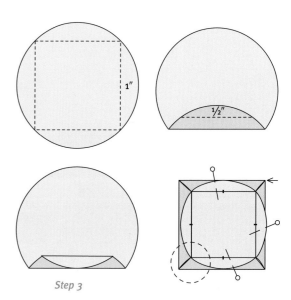

Step 3

Compositae in alternate fabrics

4. Turn over, then fold each corner to center to create new, smaller square. Manipulate fabric to allow as much as desired of contrast color to show. Stitch through all layers about ½″ (1.5 cm) from all corners. Press.

Complete

5. See pages 8–9 for directions on adding combined backing/borders. Position flowers as desired on quilt block and make tiny stitches close to center of each to hold securely in place.

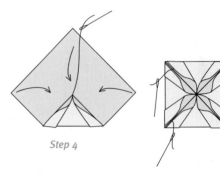

Step 4

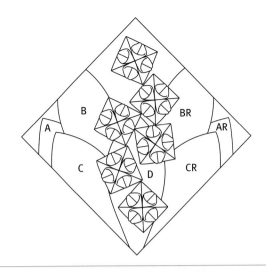

Gladiolus

1. Prepare background block following steps on page 6 and using layout diagram here as a guide. Using a ⅛″ (0.4 cm) seam allowance, appliqué leaves A to D in place in alphabetical order.

Make five flowers

2. Using square template W on page 156, cut five from each of two complementary fabrics (one dark, one light). Follow directions on page 7 to prepare squares for folding. Lightly draw diagonal guidelines on front and back of fabric square and mark center.

3. Fold each side inwards by 1¼″ (3 cm), overlapping as shown. Press firmly and pin in place. You will need to open out first corner you folded and tuck in fabric from last fold.

4. Pull out point A completely, aligning edges as shown. Make two small stitches to hold layers together at point B, stitching close to but not through base.

See templates on pages149–151. Add ⅛″ (0.4 cm) seam allowance

MATERIALS YOU WILL NEED

Base: ½ yd (45 cm)

Batting: ½ yd (45 cm)

Backing: ¾ yd (70 cm)

Appliqué leaves: ¼ yd (25 cm) each of at least three fabrics

Flower fabrics: ¼ yd (25 cm) each of at least two fabrics

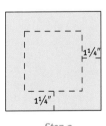
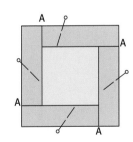

Step 3

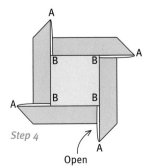

Step 4

Open

Embellished Evening Bag

Dress up a plain evening bag with any of the flowers in Flower Origami.
Or make several flowers in different colors to match the outfit you are wearing!
You'll feel as though you have a new purse every time you step out.

Gladiolus

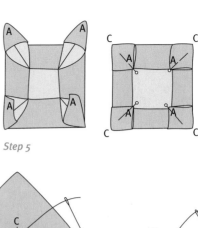

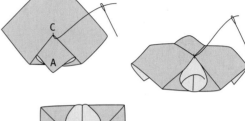

Step 5

5. Open out points A, then flatten as shown to make square at each corner. Press and pin in place.

6. Turn over. Pull one point C to center and pin in place. Repeat with second point C, diagonally opposite. Working on same two petals, pull one point A to center and make one or two stitches through all layers to hold in place. Repeat with opposite point A. Repeat entire process with remaining two points C and A.

Complete

7. See pages 8–9 for directions on adding combined backing/borders. Position flowers as desired on quilt block and, from underside, make tiny stitches at each corner to hold them securely in place.

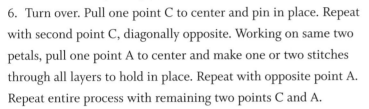

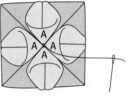

Step 6

Gladiolus Basket

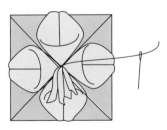

A candy basket with a difference—perfect for Easter treats or summer picnics. Or fill it with scented soaps and bath salts to add a decorative touch to the powder room. So sweet, so simple.

1. From template plastic or stiff card, prepare large square template measuring 9½″ × 9½″ (24 cm x 24 cm). Cut four each from two complementary fabrics. Follow steps 2 to 6 of *Gladiolus* on pages 101–103 to make four flowers. Stitch two strips of narrow ribbon to center of each flower.

MATERIALS YOU WILL NEED

Flower fabrics: ½ yd (45 cm) each of two different fabrics

Felt square: 4¼″ × 4¼″ (11 cm x 11 cm)

Handle: wired silk ribbon measuring 1½″ × 12″ (4 cm x 30 cm)

Yoyos: two wired silk ribbons, measuring 1½″ × 5″ (4 cm x 13 cm)

Flower centers: ¾ yd (70 cm) of narrow ¼″ (0.75 cm) ribbon cut into eight 3″ (7.5 cm) strips

Step 1

Fennel Flower *and* **Mallow Rose**

Holiday Decorations

Holiday decorations with a difference! Make any of the flower designs in seasonal colors, attach a loop of embroidery thread to the back, and display on your Christmas tree.

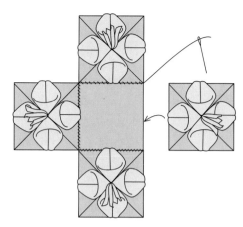

Step 2

2. Lay out completed flowers with square of felt at center. With right sides facing, use fine overcast stitches to sew one edge of each flower to felt.

3. Using coil stitch (see page 16), sew sides of adjacent flowers together to create cube.

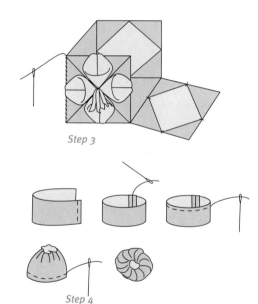

Step 3

4. For yoyos, stitch short edges of wired ribbon strips together to make loop. Turn right side out. Gather stitch along one long edge, pull stitches tight, and backstitch to hold. Gather stitch along other long edge, pulling gathers gently until diameter or opening is about ¾″ (2 cm). Backstitch to hold. Make two.

5. For handle, use length of wired ribbon. Fold each end inwards by ¼″ (0.75 cm) and overcast stitch to hold. Use your fingers to make tuck at center of each end of ribbon. Use overcast stitch to sew ends of ribbon at opposite sides of basket, exactly where two flowers join. Attach first yoyo to completely cover end of ribbon. Repeat at other end of ribbon.

Step 4

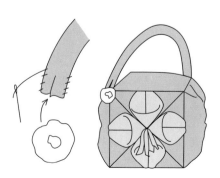

Step 5

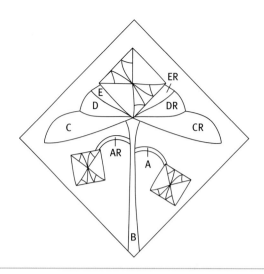

Iris

1. Prepare background base following steps on page 6 and using layout diagram here as a guide. Using ⅛″ (0.4 cm) seam allowance, appliqué leaves A and A-R, stem B, and leaves stems C, CR, D, DR, E, and ER in place in alphabetical order.

Make one large flower and two small flowers

2. Use circle template X on page 156, cut one from each of two complementary fabrics (one dark, one light). Using smaller circle template XX, cut two from each fabric. Follow directions on page 7 to prepare circles for folding. Lightly mark center of each circle, then mark horizontally across center.

3. Fold top and bottom of circle to center. Press, pin, then stitch once or twice at center to hold. At bottom, fold back top layer, aligning along bottom edge as shown. Press and pin. Repeat on opposite side and at top.

See templates on page 152.
Add ⅛″ (0.4 cm) seam allowance

MATERIALS YOU WILL NEED

Base: ½ yd (45 cm)

Batting: ½ yd (45 cm)

Backing: ¾ yd (70 cm)

Appliqué stems and leaves: scraps from various floral fabrics

Flower fabrics: ¼ yd (25 cm) each of two fabrics

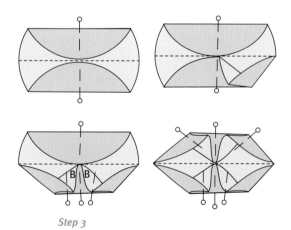

Step 3

Napkin Rings

*Origami flowers make wonderful party tokens. Dress up dinner party napkins,
then let each guest take a flower home to remember the occasion. For baby
showers or bridal showers, make each flower in soft pastels or in wedding colors*

Tangerine *and* **Fennel Flower**

Iris in alternate fabrics

4. Fold points at left and right sides inward as shown. If necessary, manipulate fabric and press again so that you have nice, sharp point at center. Press, pin, then stitch in place at center. Your finished flower should be a perfect square.

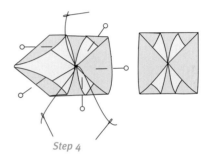

Step 4

Complete

5. See pages 8–9 for directions on adding combined backing/borders. Position flowers as desired on quilt block and, from beneath, make tiny stitches at center of each small flower and around perimeter of large flower to hold securely in place.

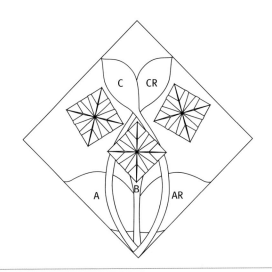

Blue Poppy

1. Prepare background base following steps on page 00 and using layout diagram here as a guide. Using ⅛" (0.4 cm) seam allowance, appliqué in place leaves A and A-R, stem B, then stems CR and C. (In photograph, stems C and C-R are made from two fabrics, joined beneath center flower to hide seams. If you decide to do same, remember to add extra seam allowance.)

Make three flowers

2. Using circle template X on page 156, cut three from each of two complementary fabrics (one dark, one light). Follow directions on page 6 to prepare circles for folding. Lightly mark center of square on both sides. Mark four points at 1⅛" (3 cm) distance from center.

3. Fold each side inwards to meet previously marked point. Press, pin, then stitch once or twice to hold.

See templates on pages 153.
Add ⅛" (0.4 cm) seam allowance

MATERIALS YOU WILL NEED

Base: ½ yd (45 cm)

Batting: ½ yd (45 cm)

Backing: ¾ yd (70 cm)

Appliqué stems and leaves: ¼ yd for leaves; scraps of complementary fabrics for stems

Flower fabrics: ¼ yd (25 cm) each of two fabrics

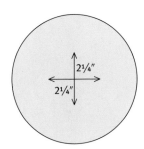

Step 2

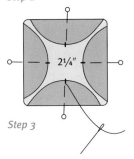

Step 3

Gift Wrap

Turn a bottle of wine into an extra-special hostess gift. Just attach the center of a length of ribbon to the back of the flower, wrap around the bottle and tie at the neck.

Tangerine

4. Fold top layer back at each corner by ½″ (1–5 cm), revealing contrast fabric and creating petal shape. Press.

5. Turn over. Fold each corner inwards and stitch to hold at center of flower.

Complete

6. See pages 8–9 for directions on adding combined backing/borders. Position flowers as desired on quilt block and make tiny stitches close to center of each to hold securely in place.

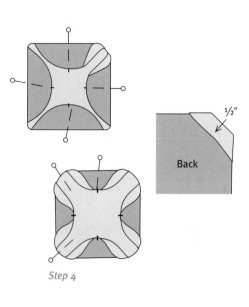

Step 4

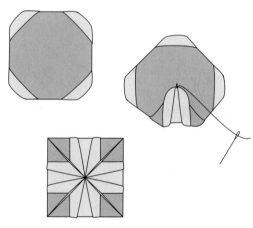

Step 5

Poinsettia Gift Box

What better way to wrap a special gift than in this beautiful hand-crafted box. Made entirely from fabric and felt, it's easy to adjust the color scheme to suit any holiday or occasion. Decorative beads at the center of each flower add extra sparkle.

1. Using circle template X on page 157, cut five from each of two complementary fabrics (one dark, one light). Follow steps 2 to 5 of *Blue Poppy* on pages 113–115 to make five flowers. Attach decorative bead to center of each flower.

2. Cut three squares of felt measuring 3½″ × 3½″ (9 cm × 9 cm). Pin then baste two squares together to form base of box. Arrange four flowers with felt at center as shown. Use fine coil stitches (see page 16) to join flowers along all four sides of felt square. Again using coil stitch, sew remaining felt square to back of last flower to form box lid.

3. Use coil stitch to attach lid to box.

4. Cut strip of felt measuring 1″ × 10½″ (2.5 cm × 27 cm). Attach around sides and front of box rim and press in place, inside box. Trim any excess felt. Pinch top front corners of box by about ¼″ (0.75 cm) and stitch to hold. This helps lid sit neatly on top of box.

MATERIALS YOU WILL NEED

Flower fabrics: ¼ yd (25 cm) each of at least two fabrics

Felt: ⅛ yd (15 cm) or scraps

5 decorative beads

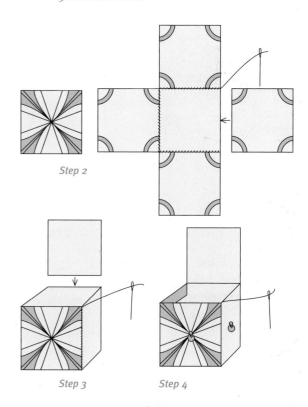

Step 2

Step 3

Step 4

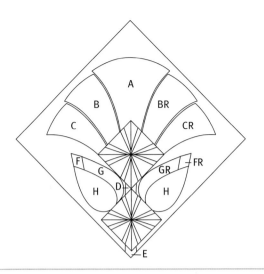

Lotus Flower

1. Prepare background base following steps on page 6 and using layout diagram as a guide. Using ⅛″ (0.4 cm) seam allowance, appliqué leaves A, B, BR, C, CR, stems D and E, then leaf pieces F, G, H and FR, GR, H in place in alphabetical order.

Make two flowers

2. Using circle template X on page 157, cut two from each of two complementary fabrics (one dark, one light). Follow directions on page 7 to prepare circles for folding. Lightly mark center of circle on both sides.

3. Fold each side inwards toward center by 1⅛″ (3 cm). Press and pin, then stitch at midpoint of each curve to hold. Fold back each curve at either side of stitched midpoint to reveal inside fabric. Press and pin, making sure all corners are sharp. You should now have a perfect square.

See templates on pages 154–155.
Add ⅛″ (0.4 cm) seam allowance

MATERIALS YOU WILL NEED

Base: ½ yd (45 cm)

Batting: ½ yd (45 cm)

Backing: ¾ yd (70 cm)

Appliqué stems and leaves: ¼ yd (25 cm) of primary leaf fabric plus scraps of complementary fabrics

Flower fabrics: ¼ yd (25 cm) each of two fabrics

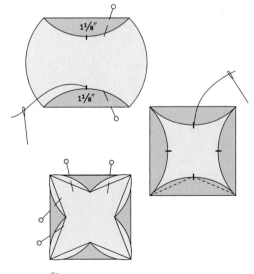

Step 3

CD Wallet

Origami flowers are so versatile they can beautifully embellish just about any item you can think of. They turn ordinary purchases like this simple CD case into extraordinary gifts.

Lotus Flower

Lotus Flower *in alternate fabrics*

4. Turn over. Fold all corners to center and stitch once or twice to hold. Press.

Complete

5. See pages 8–9 for directions on adding combined backing/ borders. Position flowers as desired on quilt block and make tiny stitches close to center to hold securely in place.

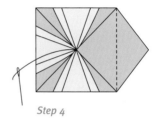

Step 4

Templates

ALL TEMPLATES ARE DRAWN TO FULL SIZE and do not
include seam allowances. If you need a guideline for
positioning templates on the background block, begin by
tracing or photocopying the templates onto template plastic,
stiff card, or freezer paper. Transfer all labels and markings.
Using tailor's chalk or another quilters' marker, lightly draw
around each one onto the background fabric. Next position
each template on the fabric from which it is to be cut. Eyeball
a ⅛" (0.4 cm) seam allowance (or the seam allowance
indicated) around all sides and cut to size. If you are
uncomfortable estimating the seam allowance, remake your
templates with the seam allowance already added in. Note
that many of the larger appliqués and some of the pieces
from the purse projects have been divided in order to fit onto
the page (see *Thistle* on page 126 or *Tangerine Tote* on page
128, for instance). Before marking or cutting, create the
complete template by taping the separate pieces together as
indicated on the template.

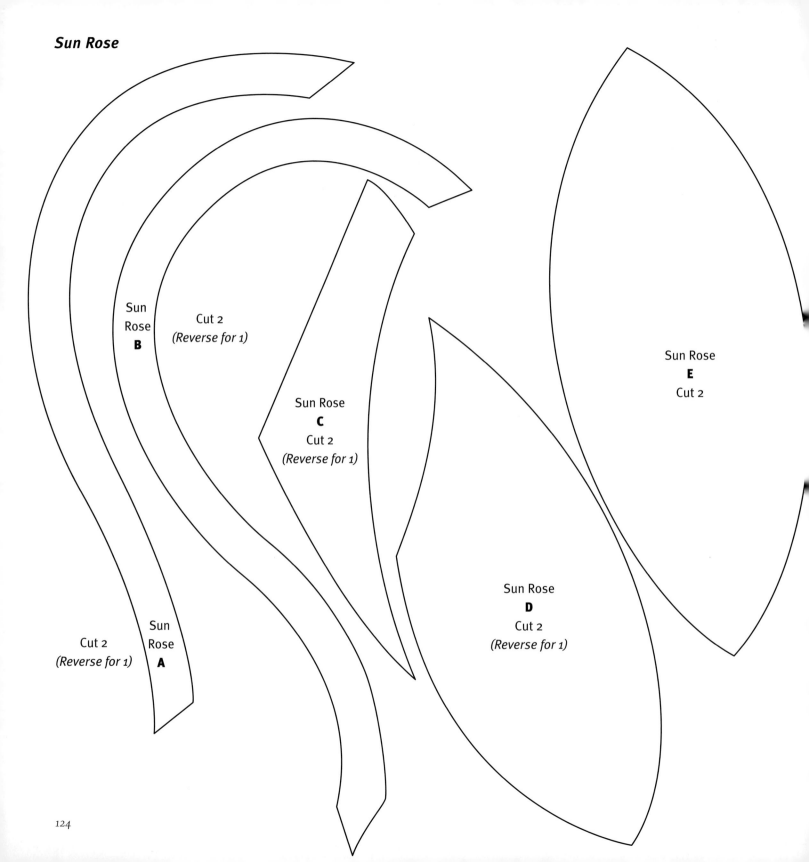

Sun Rose

Sun
Rose
B

Cut 2
(Reverse for 1)

Sun Rose
C
Cut 2
(Reverse for 1)

Sun Rose
E
Cut 2

Sun Rose
D
Cut 2
(Reverse for 1)

Cut 2
(Reverse for 1)

Sun
Rose
A

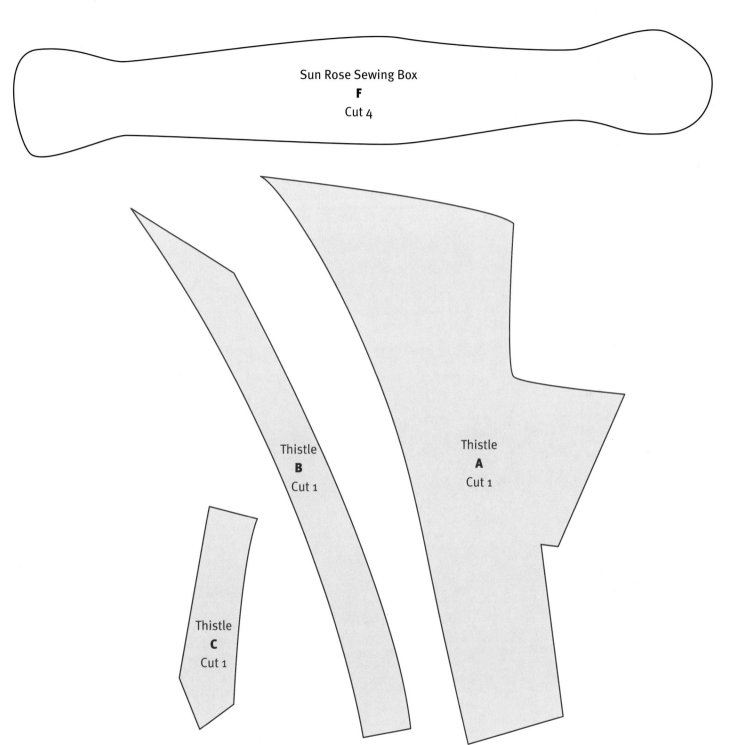

Sun Rose Sewing Box
F
Cut 4

Thistle
B
Cut 1

Thistle
A
Cut 1

Thistle
C
Cut 1

Thistle/Tangerine

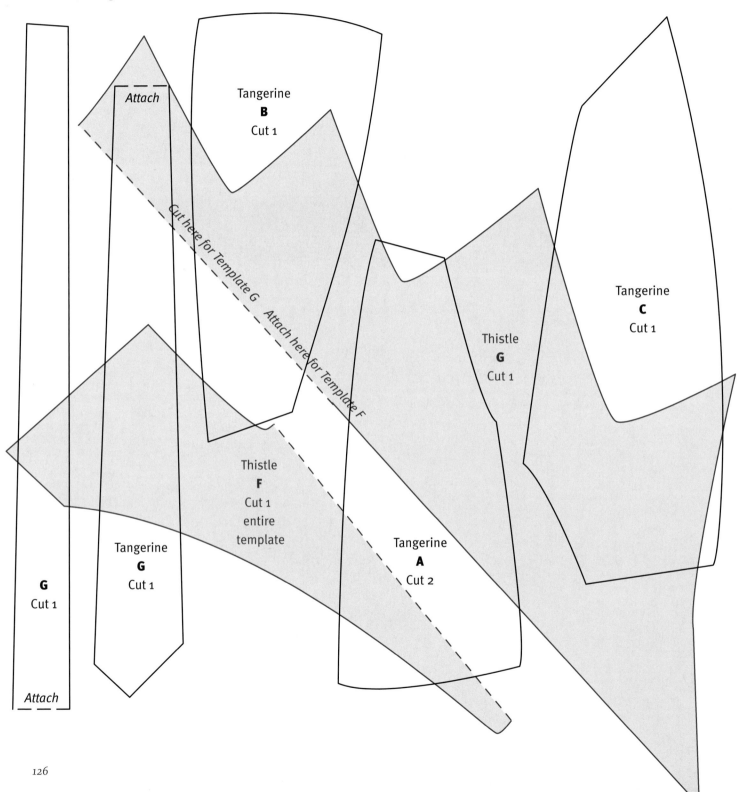

Attach

Tangerine
B
Cut 1

Cut here for Template G   Attach here for Template F

Tangerine
C
Cut 1

Thistle
G
Cut 1

Thistle
F
Cut 1
entire
template

Tangerine
G
Cut 1

Tangerine
A
Cut 2

G
Cut 1

Attach

Thistle/Tangerine

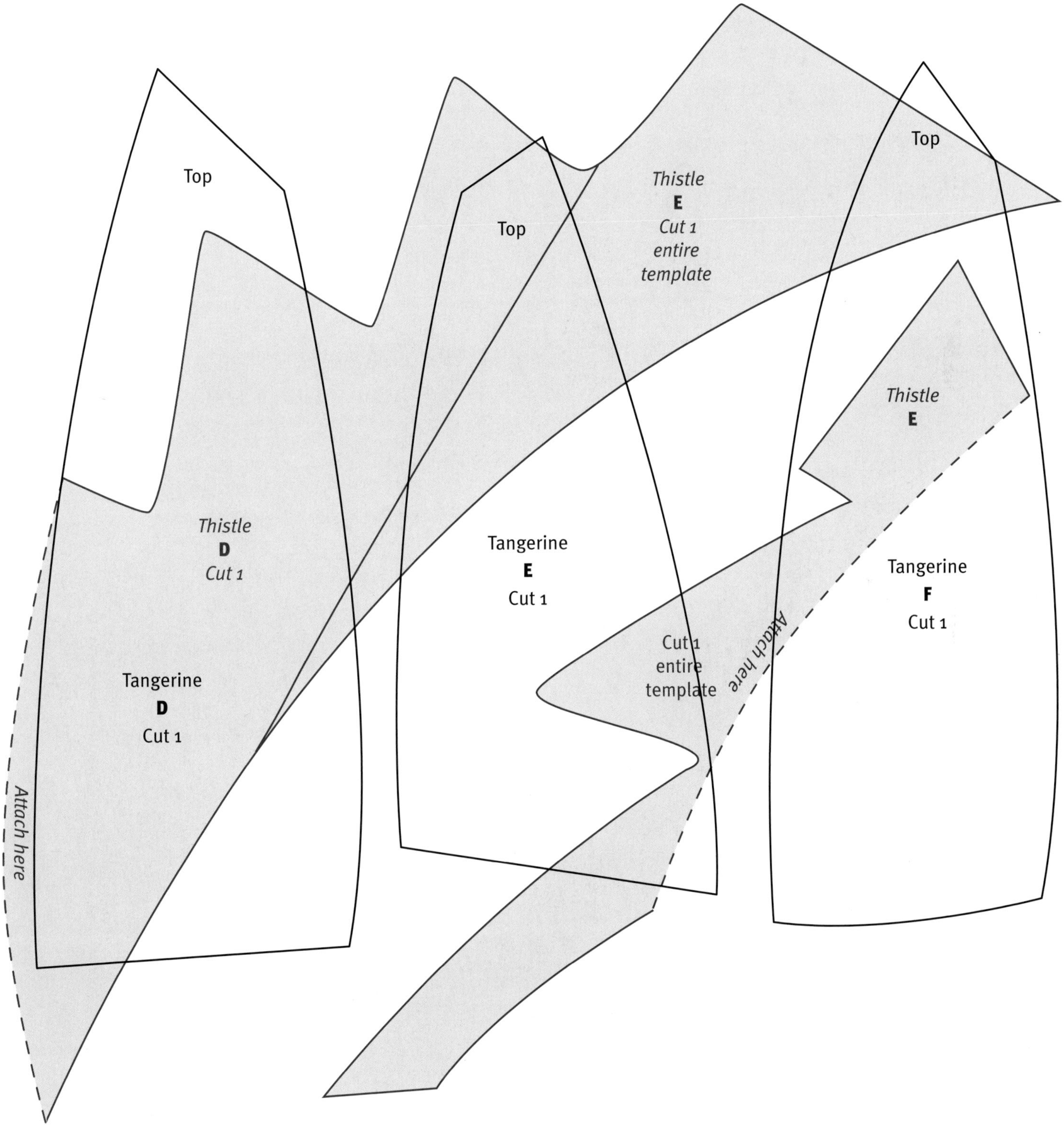
Top
Top
Top
Thistle
E
Cut 1
entire
template
Thistle
D
Cut 1
Tangerine
D
Cut 1
Tangerine
E
Cut 1
Thistle
E
Tangerine
F
Cut 1
Cut 1
entire
template
Attach here
Attach here

Tangerine Tote

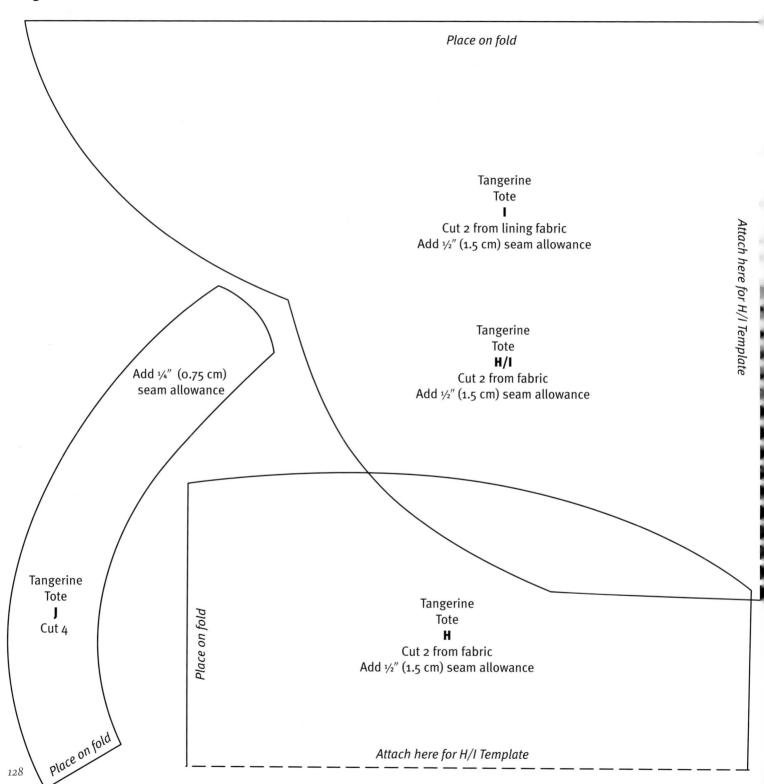

Place on fold

Tangerine
Tote
I
Cut 2 from lining fabric
Add ½″ (1.5 cm) seam allowance

Tangerine
Tote
H/I
Cut 2 from fabric
Add ½″ (1.5 cm) seam allowance

Add ¼″ (0.75 cm)
seam allowance

Tangerine
Tote
J
Cut 4

Tangerine
Tote
H
Cut 2 from fabric
Add ½″ (1.5 cm) seam allowance

Place on fold

Place on fold

Attach here for H/I Template

Attach here for H/I Template

128

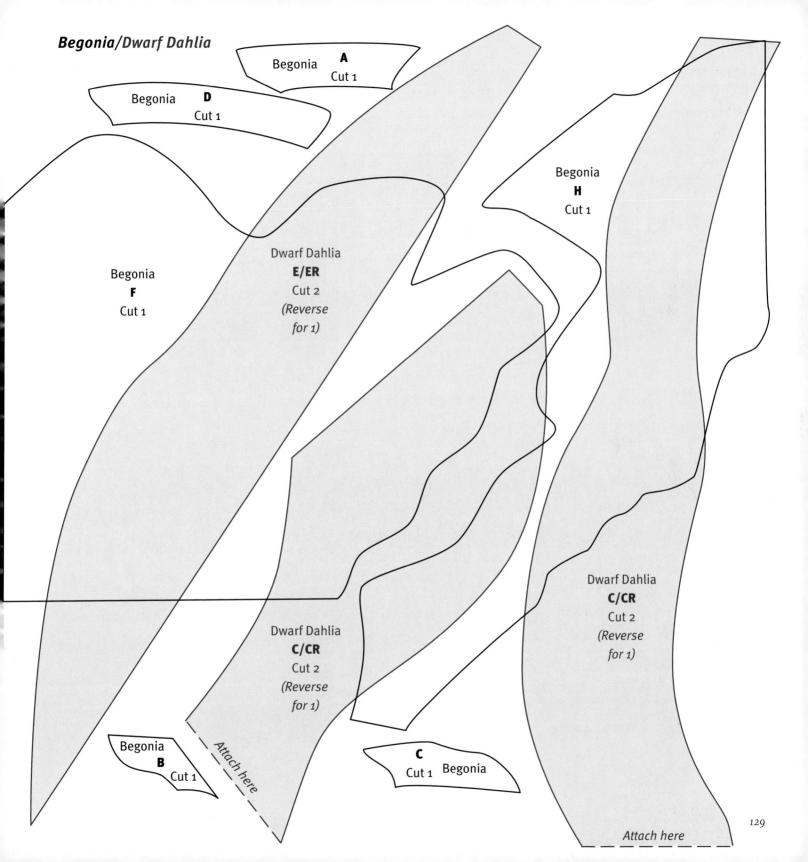

Begonia/Dwarf Dahlia

Begonia **A** Cut 1

Begonia **D** Cut 1

Begonia **F** Cut 1

Dwarf Dahlia **E/ER** Cut 2 *(Reverse for 1)*

Begonia **H** Cut 1

Dwarf Dahlia **C/CR** Cut 2 *(Reverse for 1)*

Dwarf Dahlia **C/CR** Cut 2 *(Reverse for 1)*

Begonia **B** Cut 1

Attach here

C Cut 1 Begonia

Attach here

129

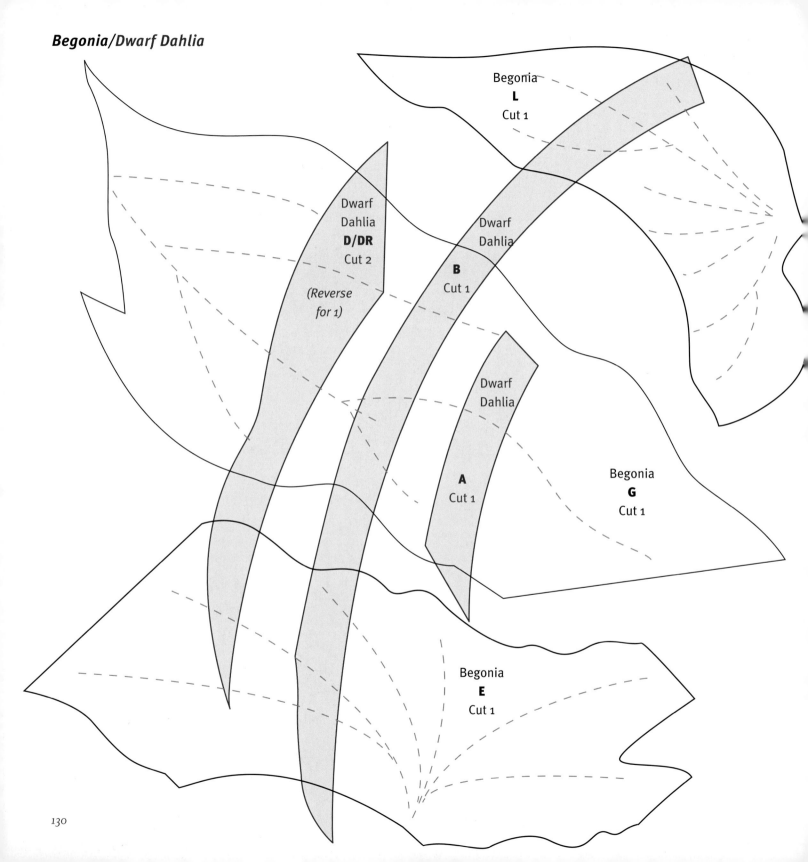

Begonia/Dwarf Dahlia

Begonia
L
Cut 1

Dwarf
Dahlia
D/DR
Cut 2

(Reverse for 1)

Dwarf
Dahlia
B
Cut 1

Dwarf
Dahlia
A
Cut 1

Begonia
G
Cut 1

Begonia
E
Cut 1

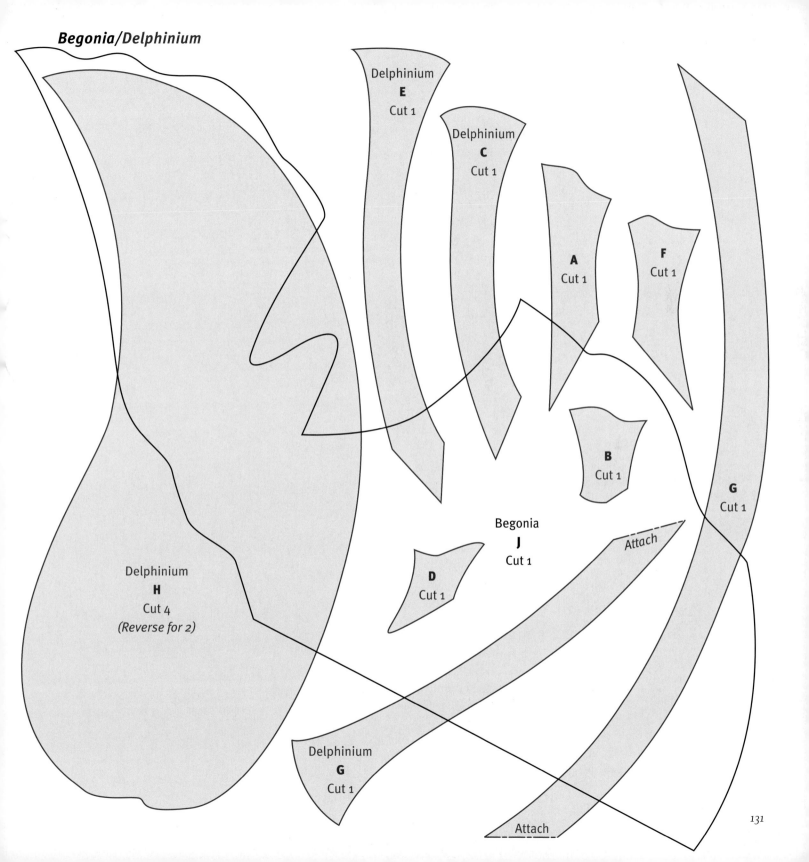

Begonia/Delphinium

Delphinium
E
Cut 1

Delphinium
C
Cut 1

Delphinium
H
Cut 4
(Reverse for 2)

A
Cut 1

F
Cut 1

B
Cut 1

G
Cut 1

Begonia
J
Cut 1

Attach

D
Cut 1

Delphinium
G
Cut 1

Attach

131

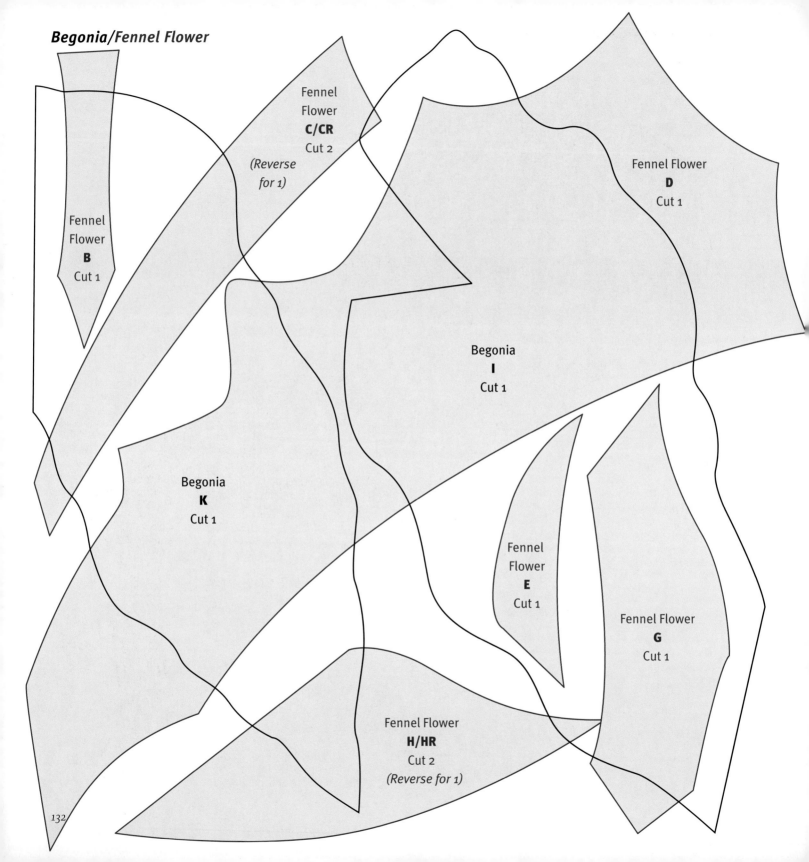

Begonia/Fennel Flower

Fennel Flower
C/CR
Cut 2
*(Reverse
for 1)*

Fennel Flower
D
Cut 1

Fennel
Flower
B
Cut 1

Begonia
I
Cut 1

Begonia
K
Cut 1

Fennel
Flower
E
Cut 1

Fennel Flower
G
Cut 1

Fennel Flower
H/HR
Cut 2
(Reverse for 1)

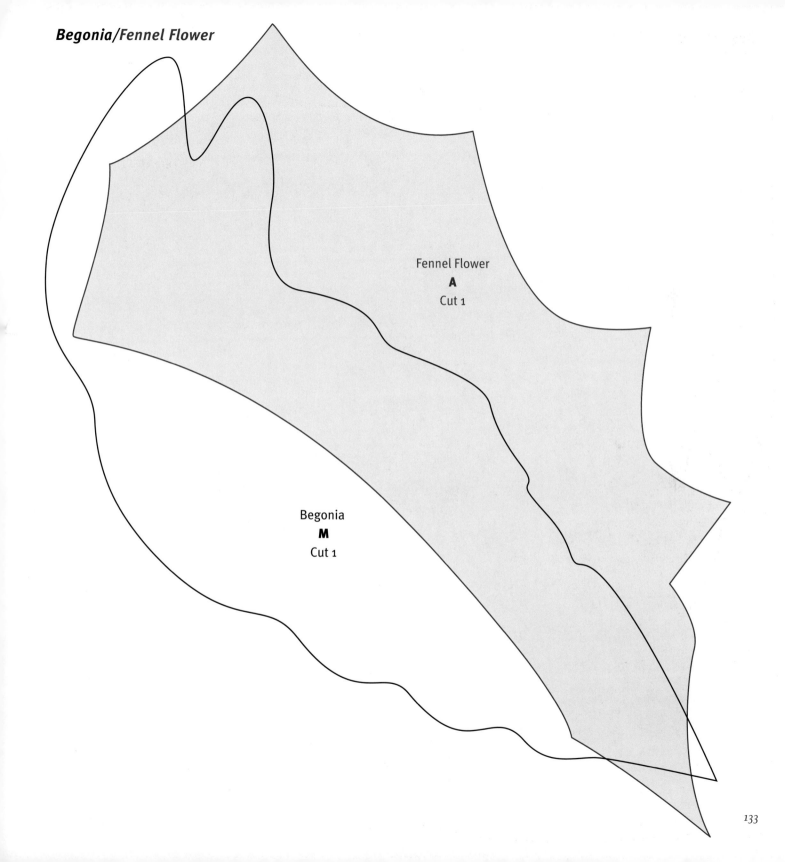

Begonia/*Fennel Flower*

Fennel Flower
A
Cut 1

Begonia
M
Cut 1

133

Fennel Flower

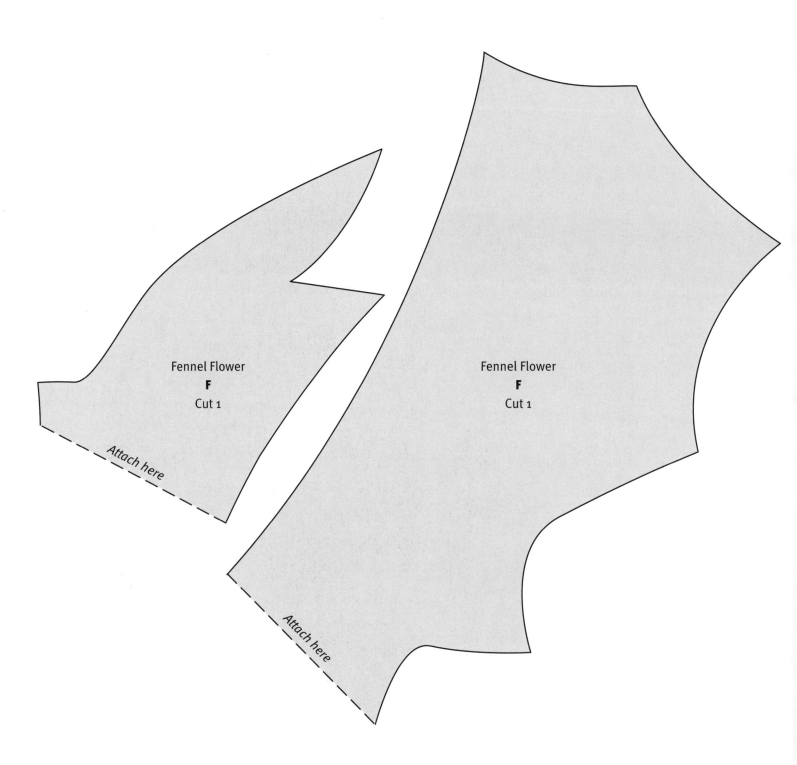

Fennel Flower
F
Cut 1

Attach here

Fennel Flower
F
Cut 1

Attach here

134

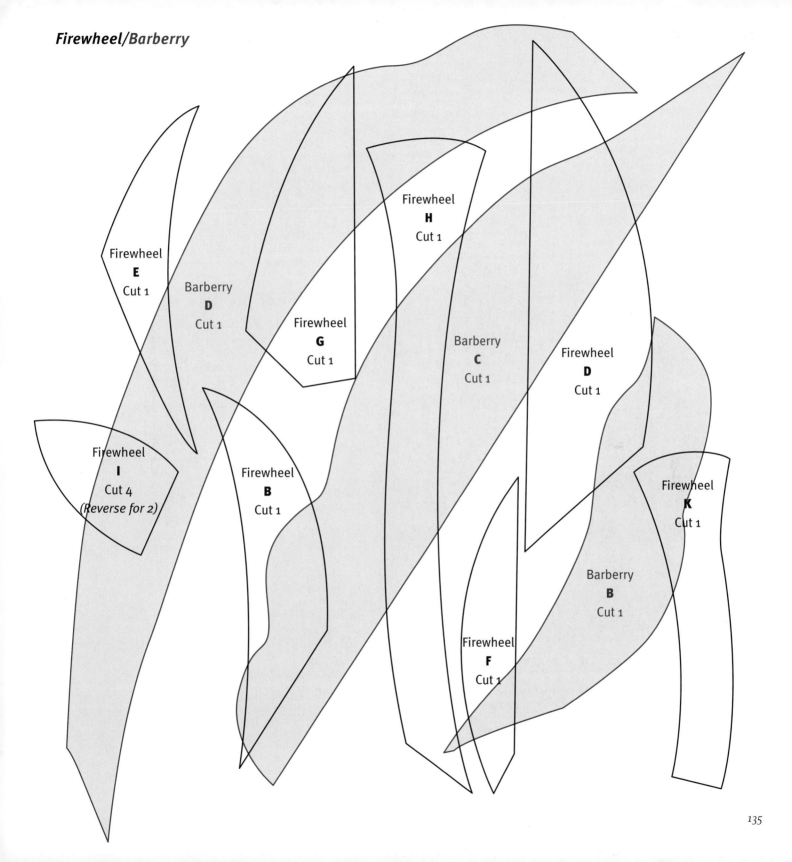

***Firewheel**/Barberry*

Firewheel
E
Cut 1

Barberry
D
Cut 1

Firewheel
H
Cut 1

Firewheel
G
Cut 1

Barberry
C
Cut 1

Firewheel
D
Cut 1

Firewheel
I
Cut 4
(Reverse for 2)

Firewheel
B
Cut 1

Firewheel
K
Cut 1

Barberry
B
Cut 1

Firewheel
F
Cut 1

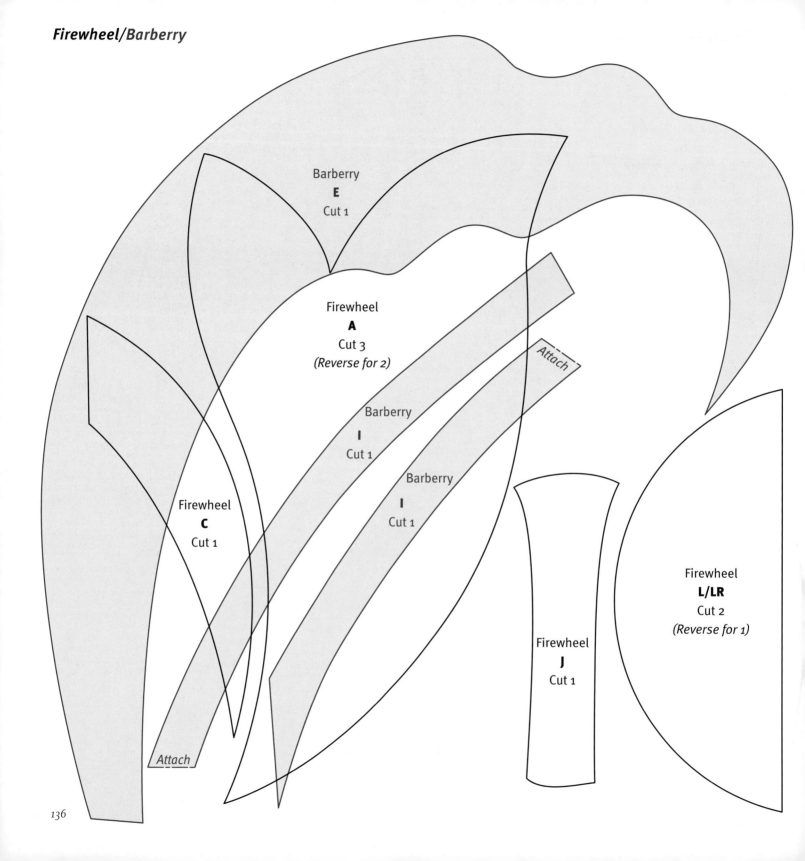

Firewheel/*Barberry*

Barberry
E
Cut 1

Firewheel
A
Cut 3
(Reverse for 2)

Attach

Barberry
I
Cut 1

Barberry
I
Cut 1

Firewheel
C
Cut 1

Firewheel
J
Cut 1

Firewheel
L/LR
Cut 2
(Reverse for 1)

Attach

Firewheel/Barberry

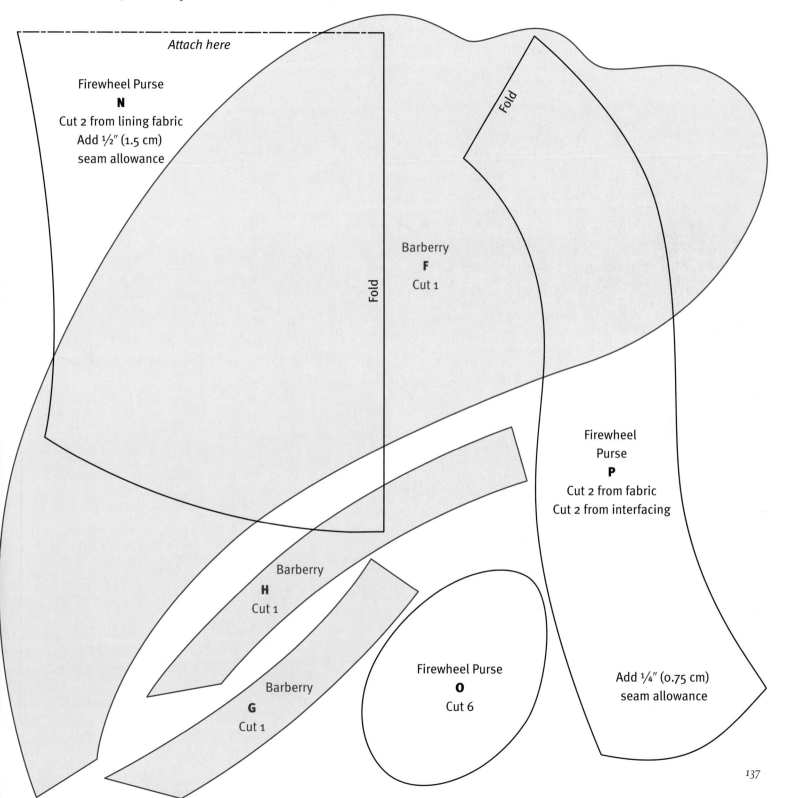

Attach here

Firewheel Purse
N
Cut 2 from lining fabric
Add ½″ (1.5 cm)
seam allowance

Fold

Barberry
F
Cut 1

Fold

Firewheel
Purse
P
Cut 2 from fabric
Cut 2 from interfacing

Barberry
H
Cut 1

Barberry
G
Cut 1

Firewheel Purse
O
Cut 6

Add ¼″ (0.75 cm)
seam allowance

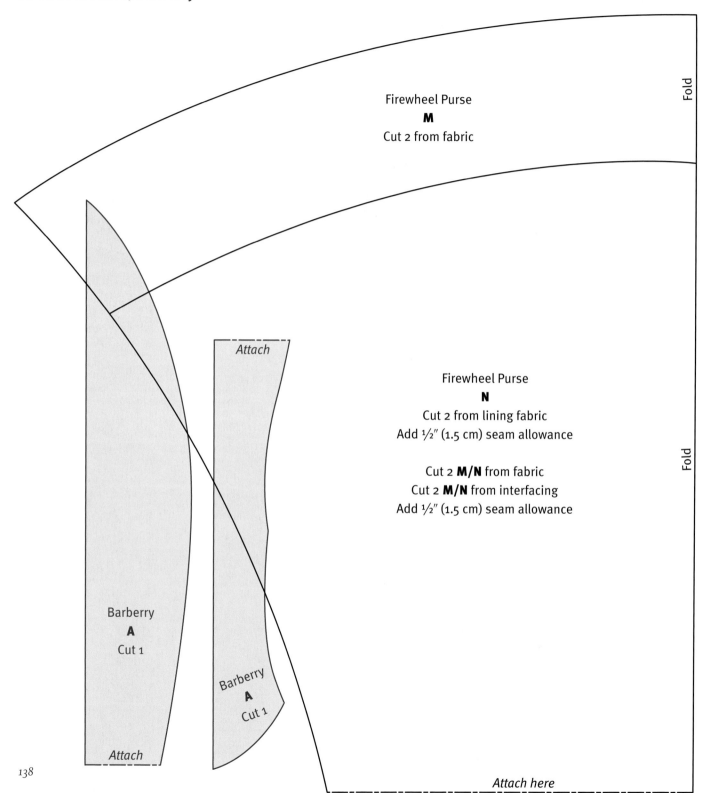

Fold

Firewheel Purse

M

Cut 2 from fabric

Attach

Firewheel Purse

N

Cut 2 from lining fabric

Add ½″ (1.5 cm) seam allowance

Cut 2 **M/N** from fabric

Cut 2 **M/N** from interfacing

Add ½″ (1.5 cm) seam allowance

Fold

Barberry

A

Cut 1

Attach

Barberry

A

Cut 1

Attach here

Gloriosa Daisy

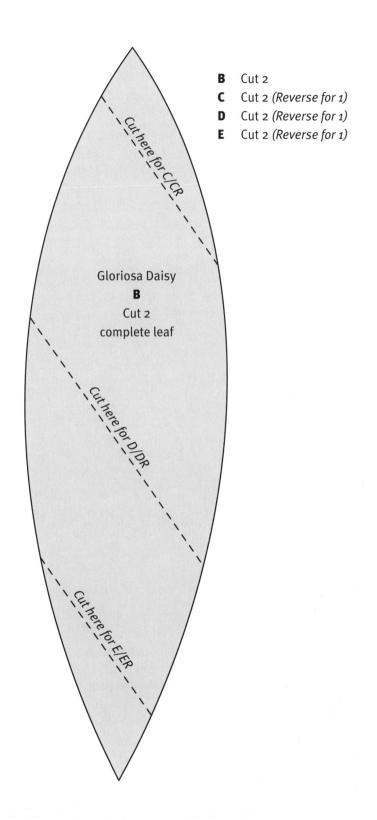

Cut here for C/CR

Gloriosa Daisy
B
Cut 2
complete leaf

Cut here for D/DR

Cut here for E/ER

B   Cut 2
C   Cut 2 *(Reverse for 1)*
D   Cut 2 *(Reverse for 1)*
E   Cut 2 *(Reverse for 1)*

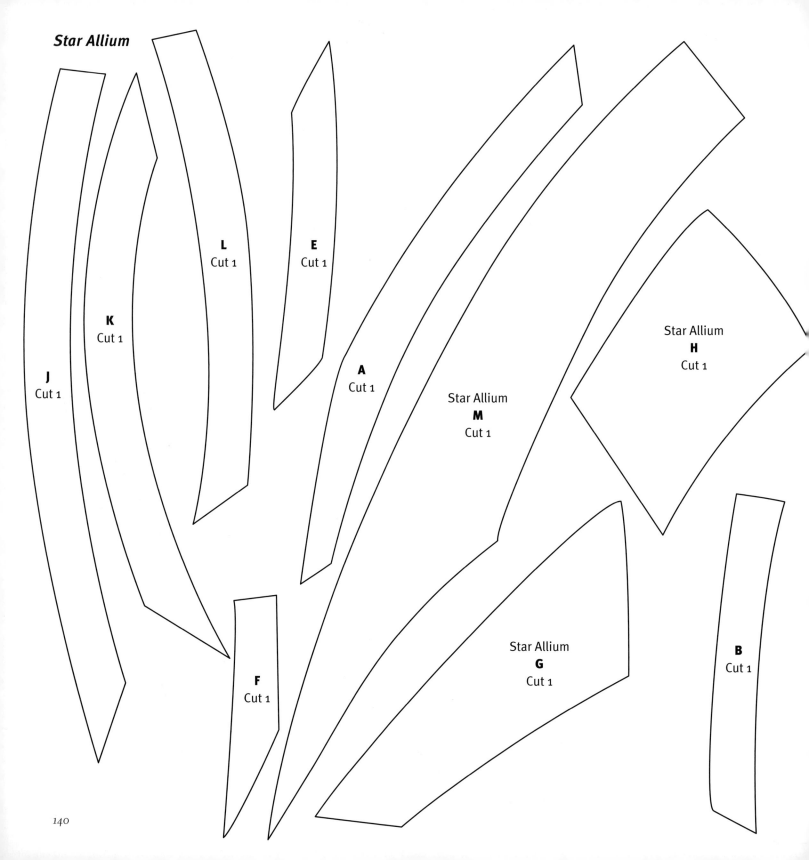

Star Allium

L
Cut 1

E
Cut 1

K
Cut 1

J
Cut 1

A
Cut 1

Star Allium
M
Cut 1

Star Allium
H
Cut 1

F
Cut 1

Star Allium
G
Cut 1

B
Cut 1

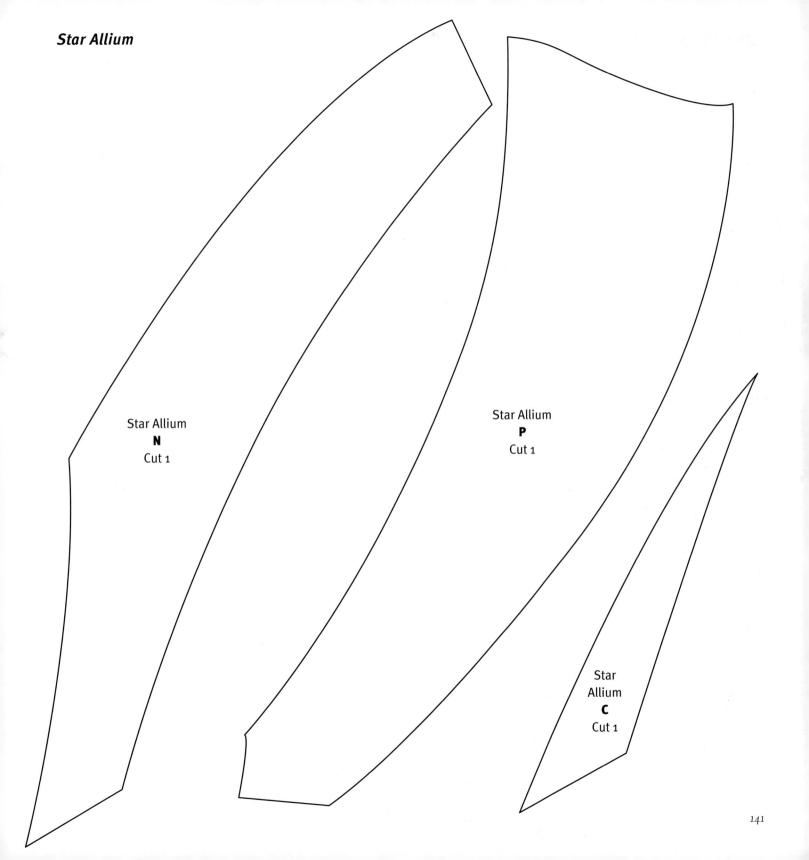

Star Allium

Star Allium
N
Cut 1

Star Allium
P
Cut 1

Star
Allium
C
Cut 1

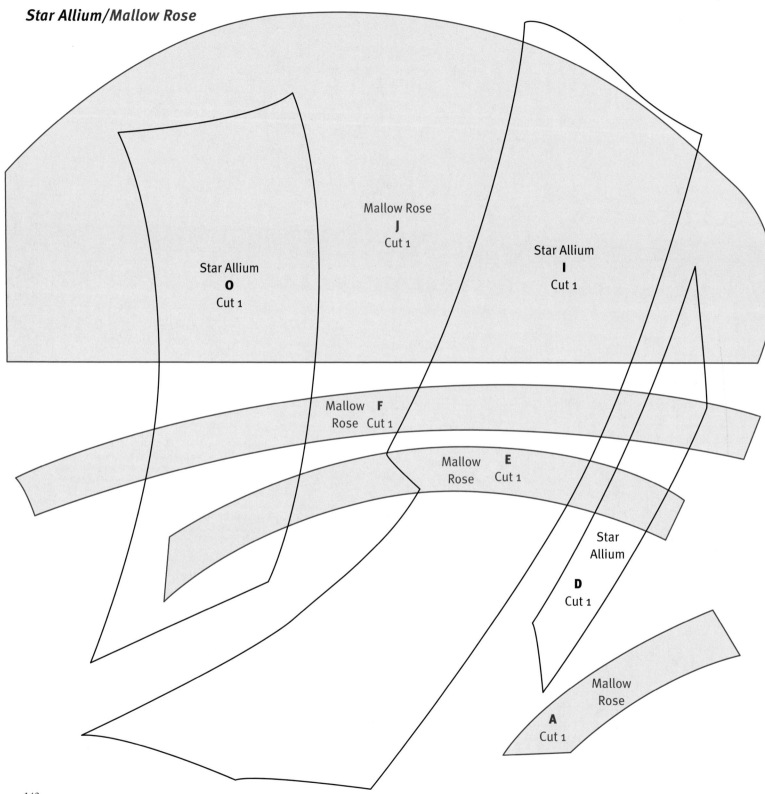

Star Allium/Mallow Rose

Mallow Rose
J
Cut 1

Star Allium
I
Cut 1

Star Allium
O
Cut 1

Mallow **F**
Rose Cut 1

Mallow **E**
Rose Cut 1

Star
Allium
D
Cut 1

Mallow
Rose
A
Cut 1

Mallow Rose

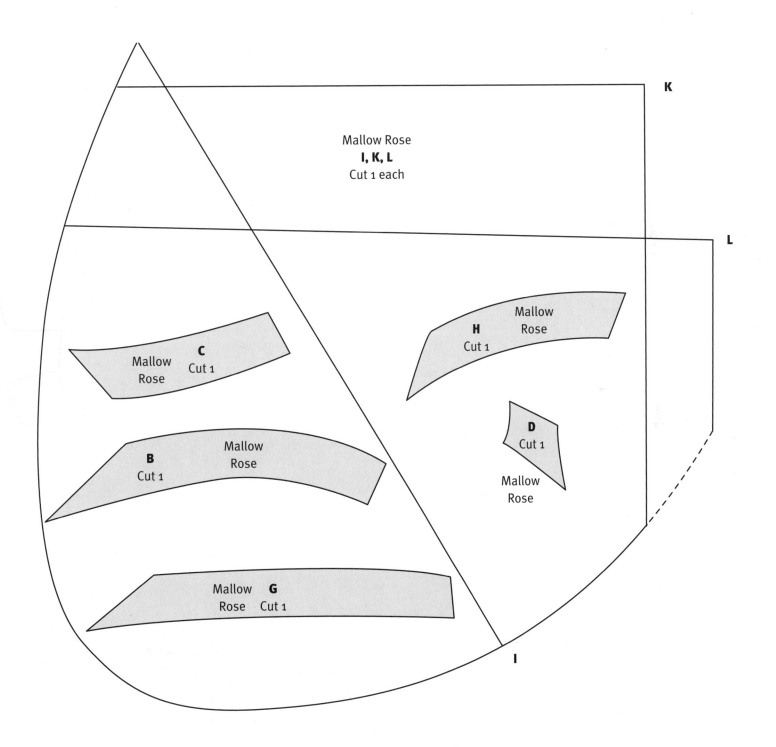

Mallow Rose
I, K, L
Cut 1 each

K

L

Mallow
C
Rose   Cut 1

Mallow
H
Rose
Cut 1

Mallow   **D**
Rose   Cut 1

Mallow
Rose

B
Cut 1

Mallow
Rose

Mallow   **G**
Rose   Cut 1

I

Dwarf Primrose/Wild Poppy

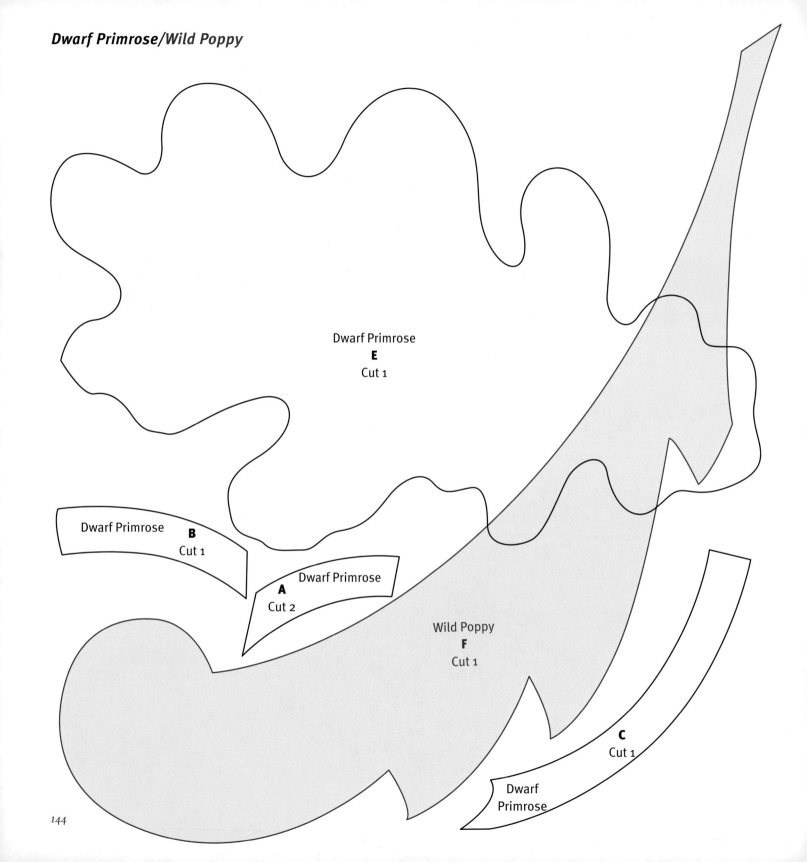

Dwarf Primrose
E
Cut 1

Dwarf Primrose
B
Cut 1

Dwarf Primrose
A
Cut 2

Wild Poppy
F
Cut 1

C
Cut 1

Dwarf
Primrose

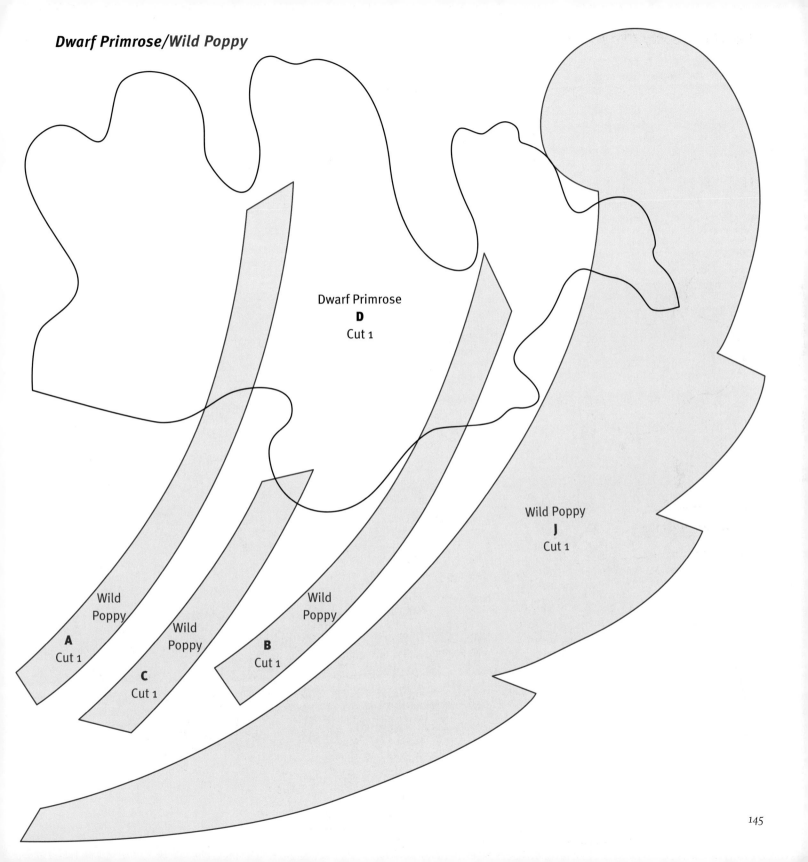

Dwarf Primrose/Wild Poppy

Dwarf Primrose
D
Cut 1

Wild Poppy
J
Cut 1

Wild Poppy
A
Cut 1

Wild Poppy
C
Cut 1

Wild Poppy
B
Cut 1

145

Wild Poppy

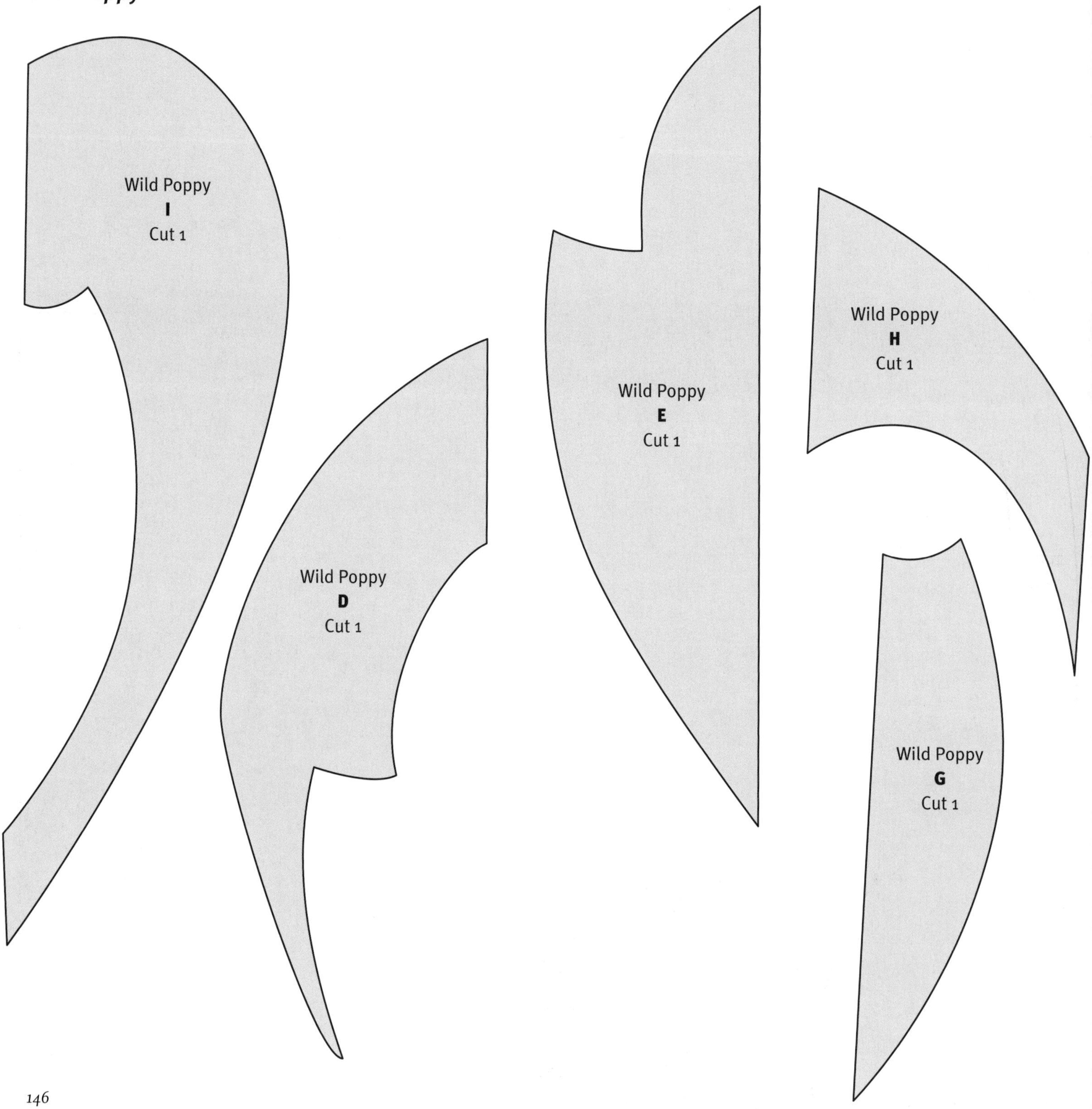

Wild Poppy
I
Cut 1

Wild Poppy
D
Cut 1

Wild Poppy
E
Cut 1

Wild Poppy
H
Cut 1

Wild Poppy
G
Cut 1

Tulip Tree

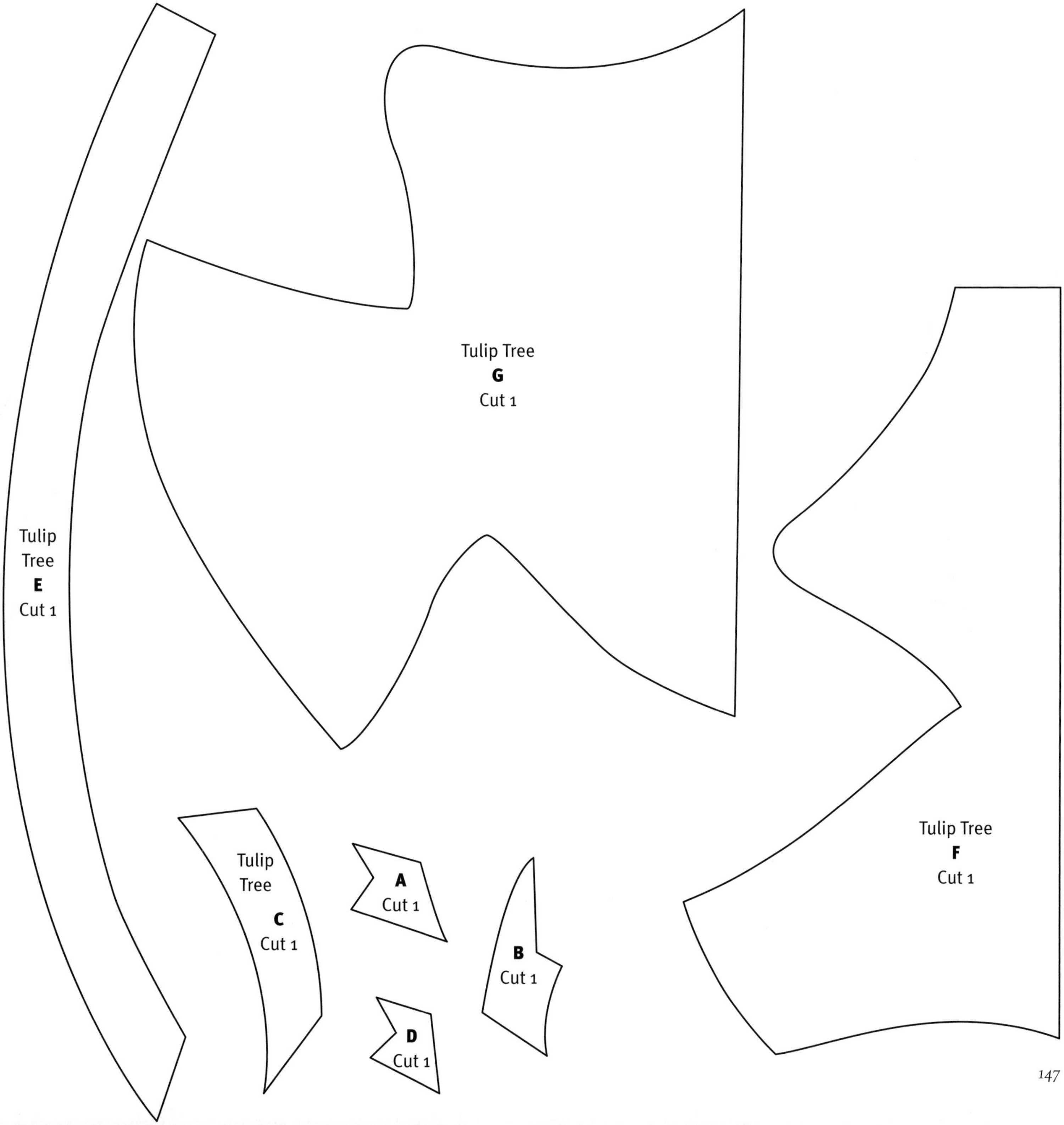

Tulip Tree
G
Cut 1

Tulip
Tree
E
Cut 1

Tulip
Tree
C
Cut 1

A
Cut 1

B
Cut 1

D
Cut 1

Tulip Tree
F
Cut 1

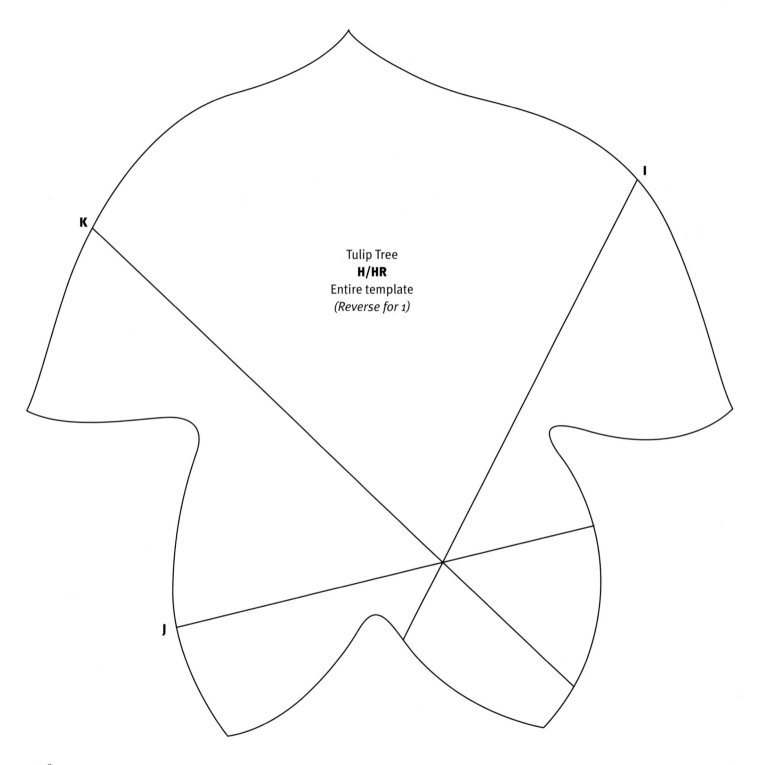

Tulip Tree
H/HR
Entire template
(Reverse for 1)

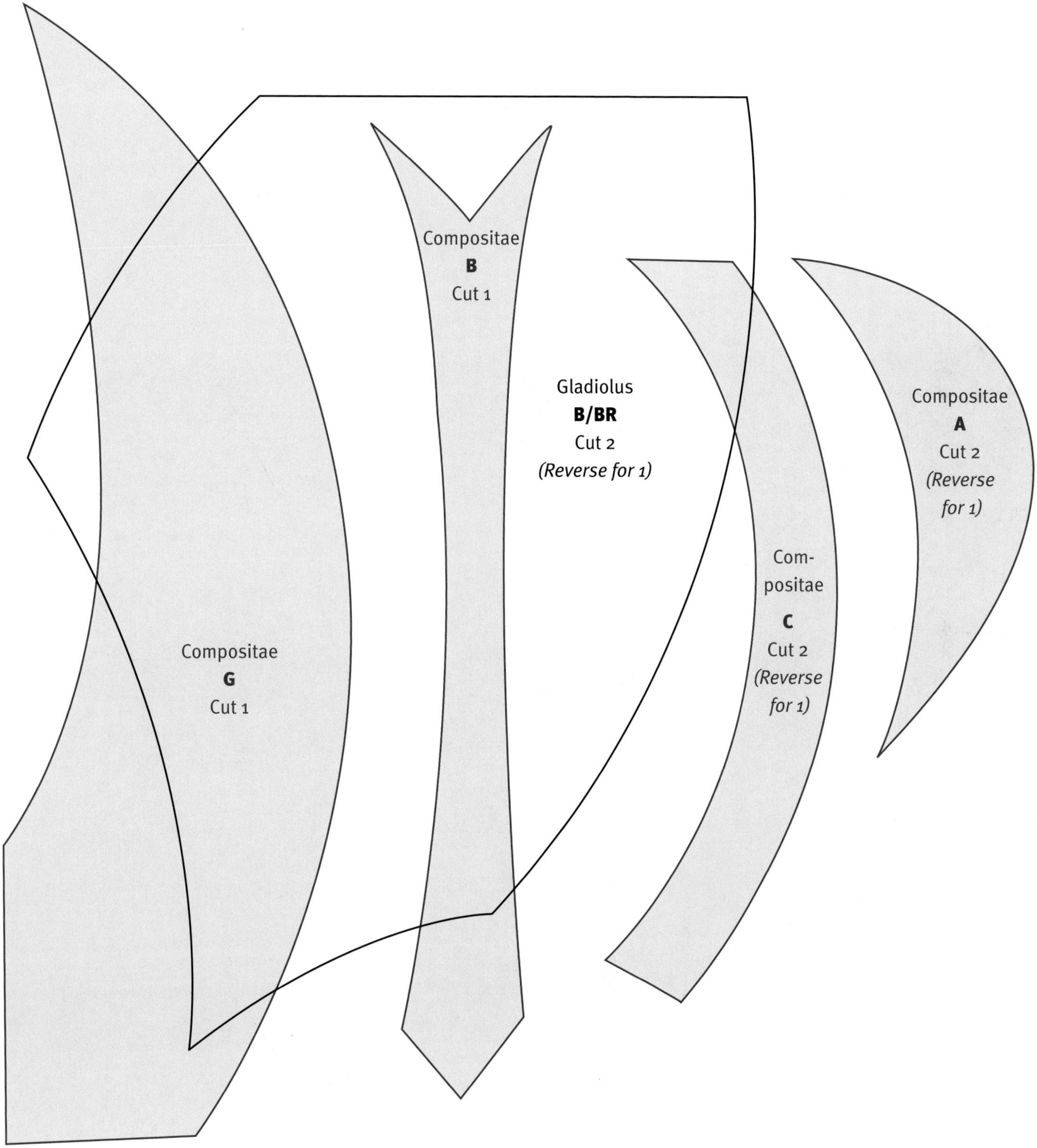

Gladiolus/Compositae

Compositae
B
Cut 1

Gladiolus
B/BR
Cut 2
(Reverse for 1)

Compositae
A
Cut 2
(Reverse for 1)

Com-
positae
C
Cut 2
(Reverse for 1)

Compositae
G
Cut 1

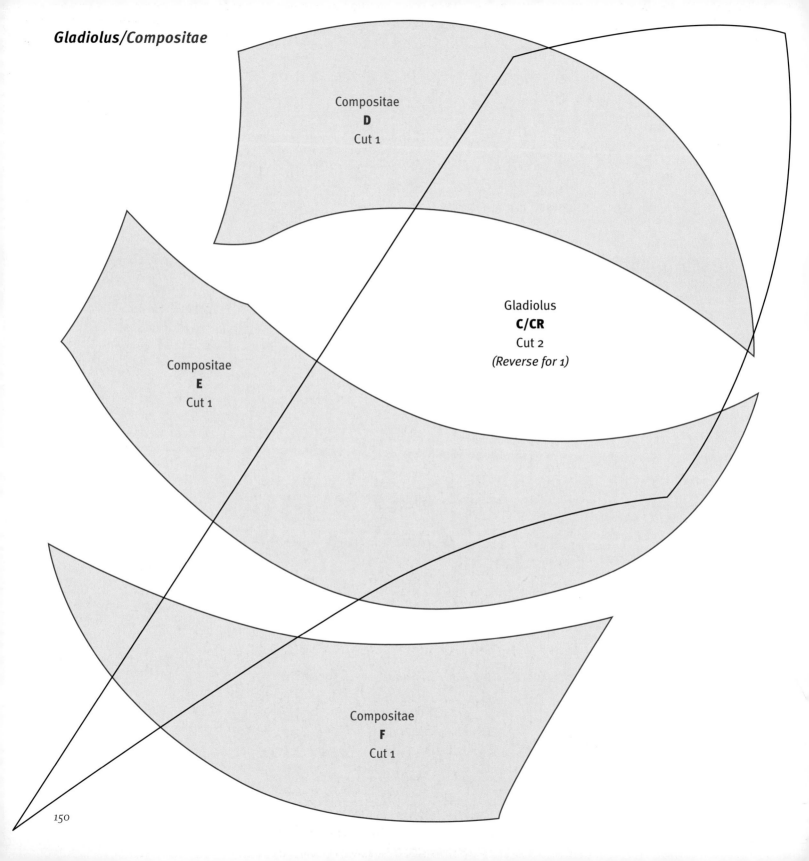

Gladiolus/Compositae

Compositae
D
Cut 1

Gladiolus
C/CR
Cut 2
(Reverse for 1)

Compositae
E
Cut 1

Compositae
F
Cut 1

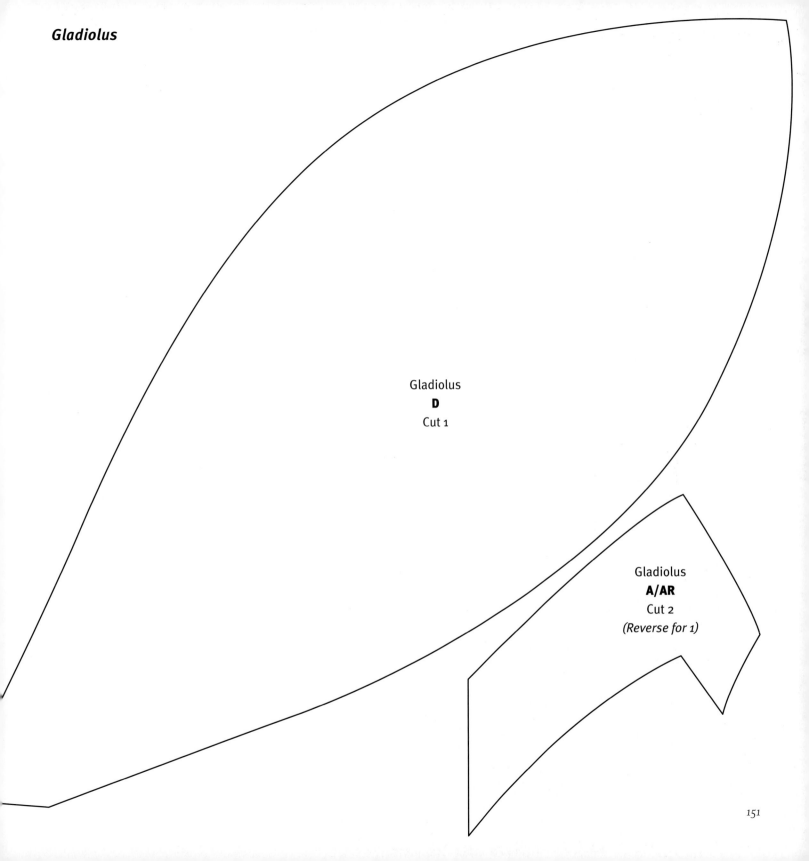

Gladiolus

Gladiolus
D
Cut 1

Gladiolus
A/AR
Cut 2
(Reverse for 1)

151

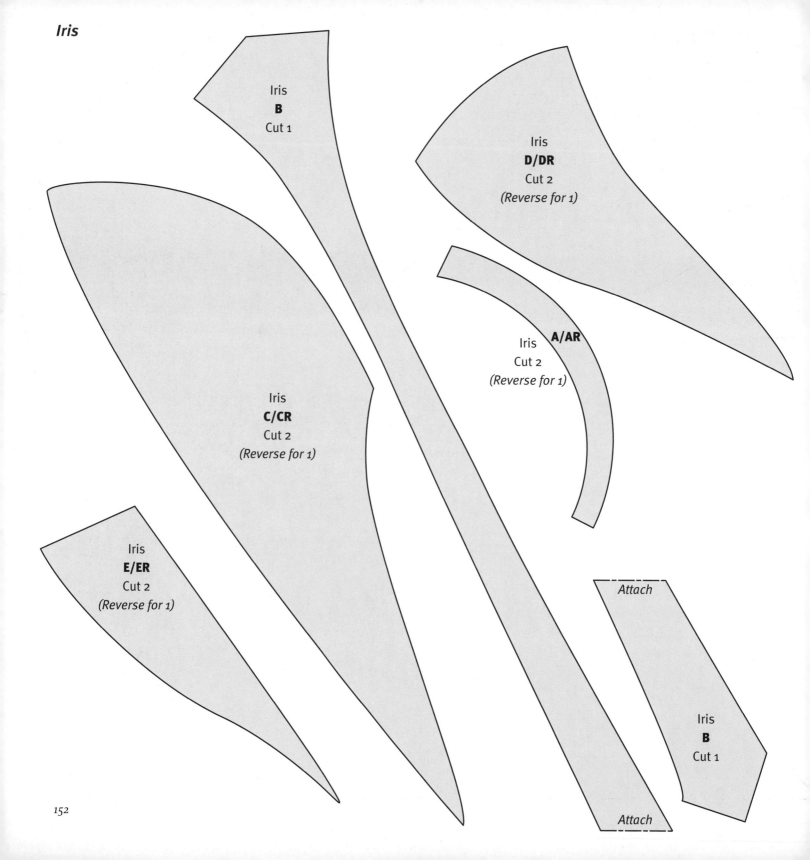

Iris

Iris
B
Cut 1

Iris
D/DR
Cut 2
(Reverse for 1)

Iris
A/AR
Cut 2
(Reverse for 1)

Iris
C/CR
Cut 2
(Reverse for 1)

Iris
E/ER
Cut 2
(Reverse for 1)

Attach

Iris
B
Cut 1

Attach

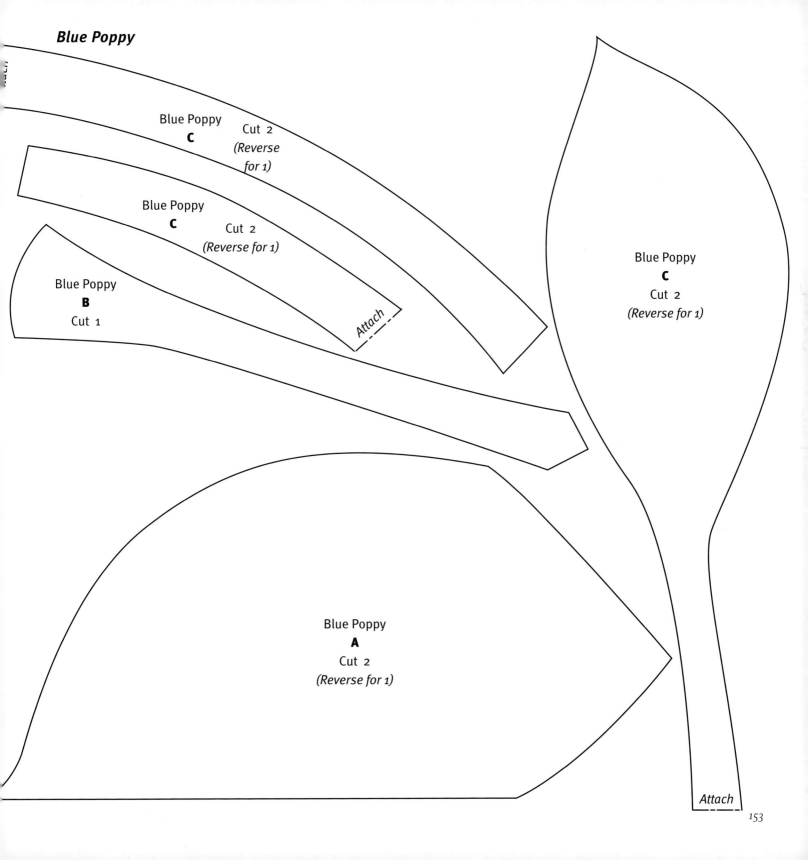

Blue Poppy

Blue Poppy
C
Cut 2
(Reverse for 1)

Blue Poppy
C
Cut 2
(Reverse for 1)

Blue Poppy
B
Cut 1

Attach

Blue Poppy
C
Cut 2
(Reverse for 1)

Blue Poppy
A
Cut 2
(Reverse for 1)

Attach

153

Lotus Flower

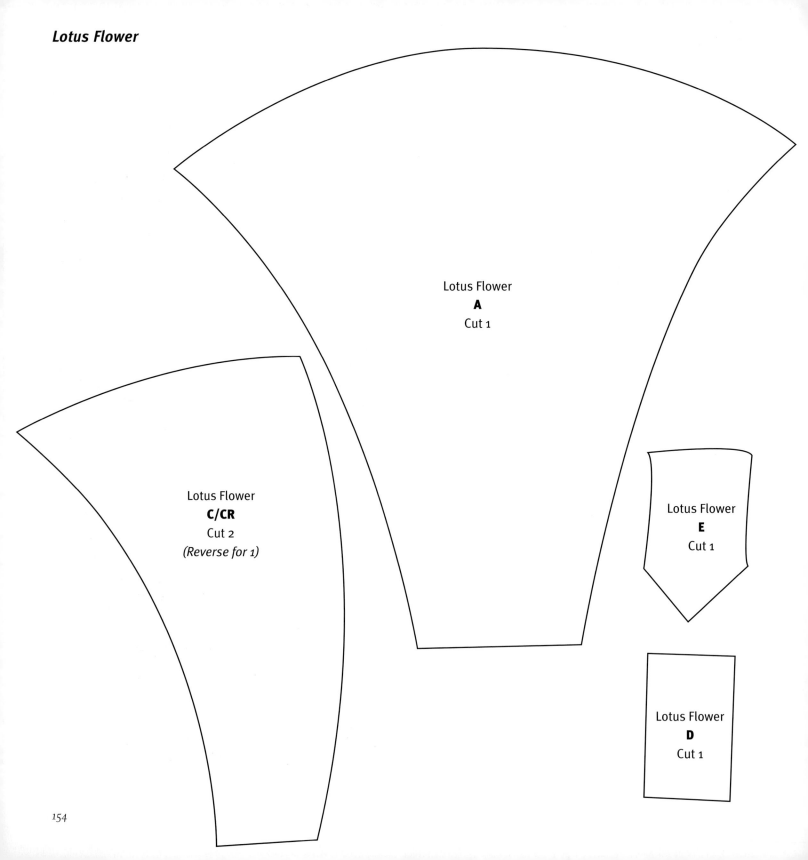

Lotus Flower
A
Cut 1

Lotus Flower
C/CR
Cut 2
(Reverse for 1)

Lotus Flower
E
Cut 1

Lotus Flower
D
Cut 1

Lotus Flower

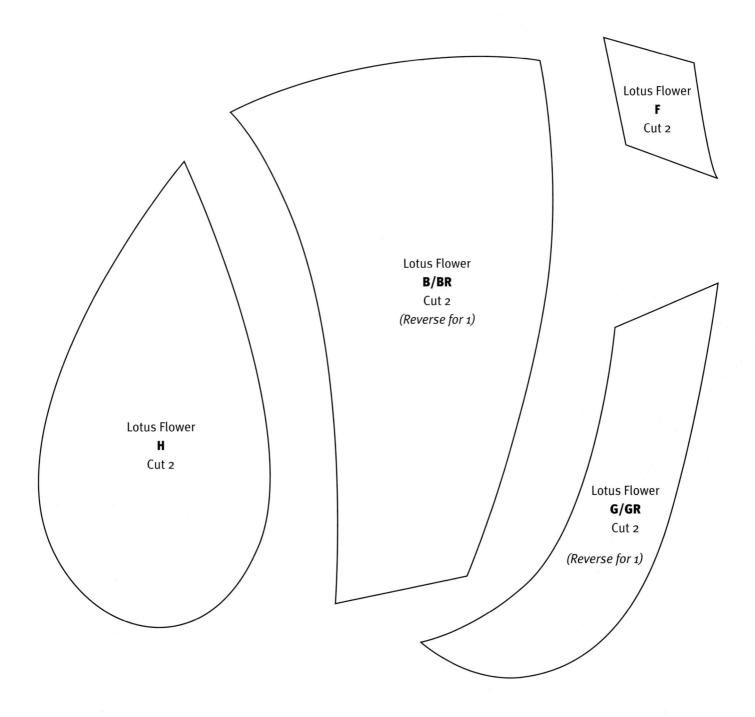

Lotus Flower
F
Cut 2

Lotus Flower
B/BR
Cut 2
(Reverse for 1)

Lotus Flower
H
Cut 2

Lotus Flower
G/GR
Cut 2

(Reverse for 1)

Square

Square Template

W

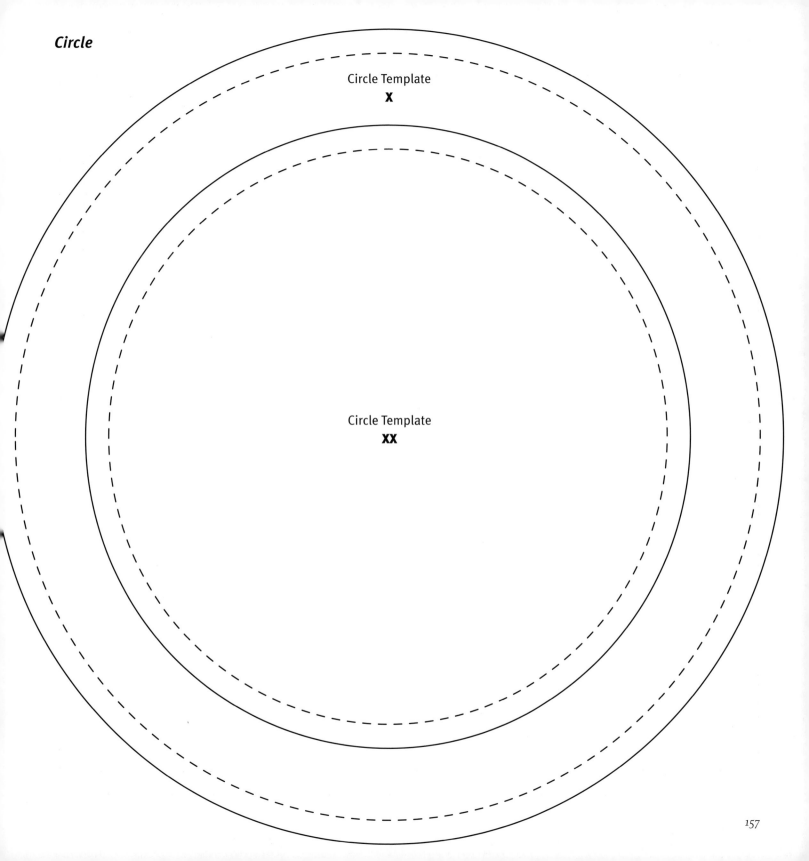

Circle

Circle Template
X

Circle Template
XX

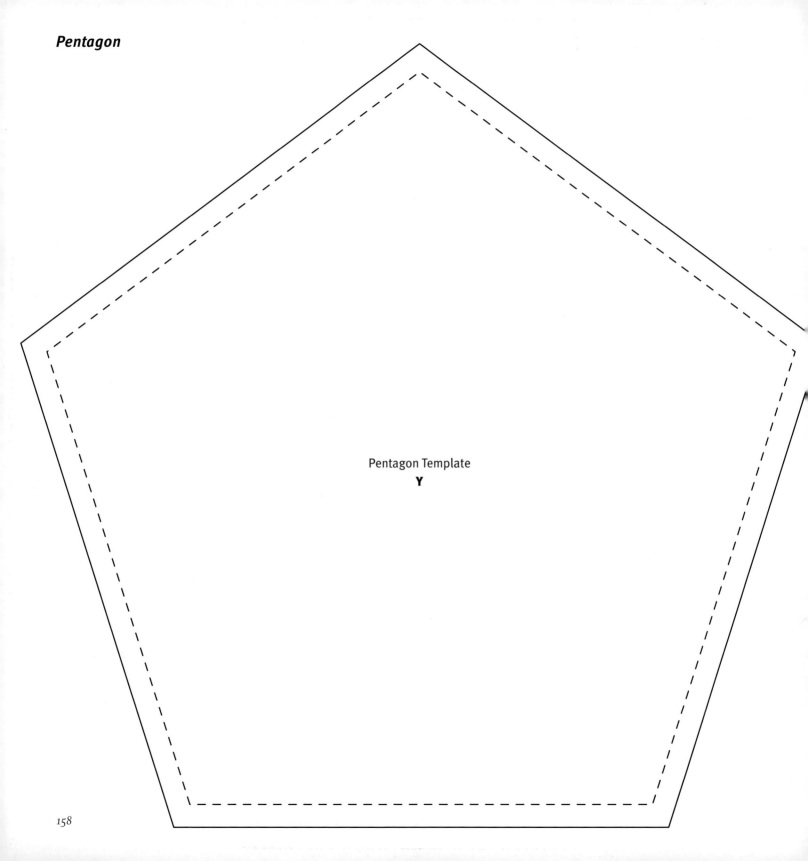

Pentagon

Pentagon Template
Y

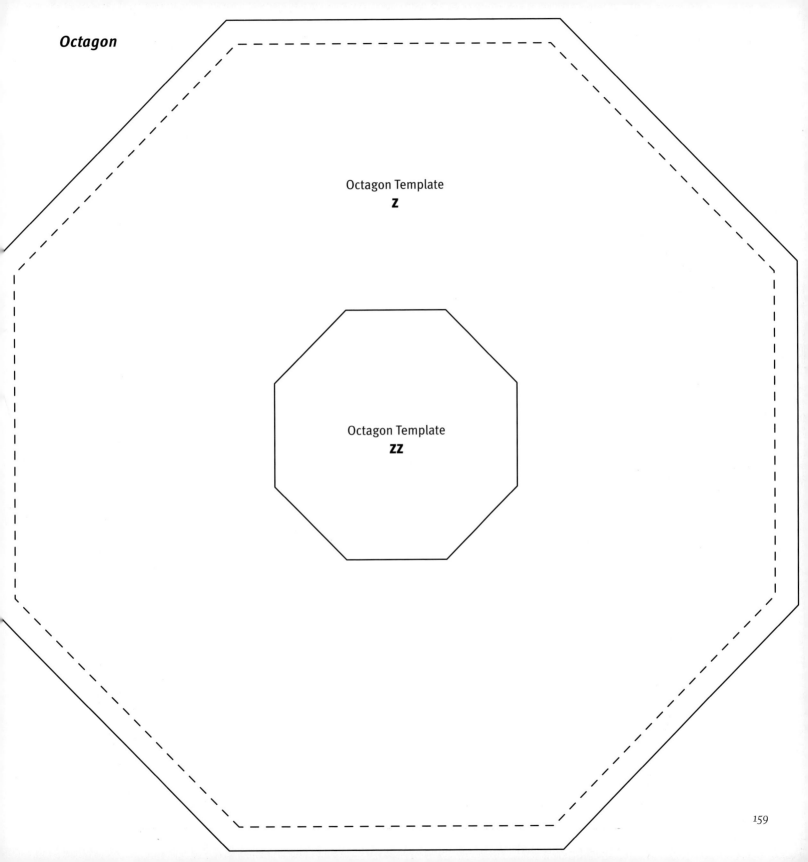

Octagon

Octagon Template
Z

Octagon Template
ZZ

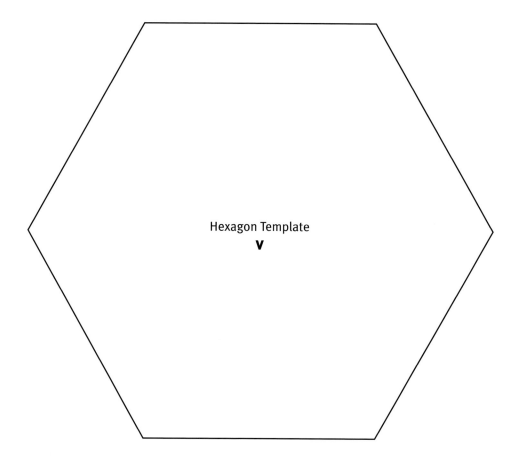

Hexagon Template
V